Journey into Depth

The Experience of Initiation in Monastic and Jungian Training

Mary Wolff-Salin

A Michael Glazier Book

LITURGICAL PRESS
Collegeville, Minnesota

www.litpress.org

Cover design by Joachim Rhoades, O.S.B. Cover art courtesy of Getty Images.

The author acknowledges with thanks the following publishers for permission to reprint the texts noted below:

Excerpt from TAO TE CHING BY LAO TZU, A NEW ENGLISH VERSION, WITH FOREWORD AND NOTES by STEPHEN MITCHELL. Translation copyright © 1988 by Stephen Mitchell. Reprinted by permission of HarperCollins Publishers Inc.

Excerpt from "The Dry Salvages" in FOUR QUARTETS, copyright 1941 by T.S. Eliot and renewed 1969 by Esme Valerie Eliot, reprinted by permission of Harcourt, Inc.

Excerpts reprinted by permission from *Magnificent One,* Selected New Verses from Divan-i Kebir of Mevlana Jalaluddin Rumi, © 1993, translated by Nevit Oguz Ergin.

Excerpts from *The Collected Works of St. John of the Cross,* translated by Kieran Kavanaugh and Otilio Rodriguez. Copyright © 1964, 1979, 1991 by Washington Province of Discalced Carmelites, ICS Publications, 2131 Lincoln Road, N.E., Washington, DC 20002-1199 U.S.A. www.icspublications.org.

The Scripture quotations contained herein are from the New Revised Standard Version Bible, Catholic Anglicized Edition, © 1999, 1995, 1989, Division of Christian Education of the National Council of the Churches of Christ in the United States of America, and are used by permission. All rights reserved.

1   2   3   4   5   6   7   8

Library of Congress Cataloging-in-Publication Data

Wolff-Salin, Mary.
    Journey into depth : the experience of initiation in monastic and Jungian training / Mary Wolff-Salin.
        p.   cm.
    "A Michael Glazier book."
    Includes bibliographical references and index.
    ISBN 13: 978-0-8146-5215-2 (alk. paper)
    ISBN 10: 0-8146-5215-8 (alk. paper)
    1. Monastic and religious life—Psychology.   2. Psychoanalysis—Study and teaching.   3. Jungian psychology.   4. Initiation rites.   I. Title.

BX2440.W64   2005
248.8'94'019—dc22   2004015392

For PE, MB, SM, FT, FS,
who have walked these ways

CONTENTS

Acknowledgments   vii

Preface   ix

Introduction   xiii

PART ONE: MONASTIC INITIATION

Section One: Anthropological Reflections on Initiation   3

Section Two: A Monastic Journal   8

    Introduction   8

    Journal   8

Section Three: Commentaries   29

    A Monastic Commentary   29

        Digression: Monastic Obedience, Celibacy, Ascesis   35

        The Aim of It All: John Cassian   37

    Anthropological Commentary   38

    Psychological Commentary   40

        Fundamental Monastic Archetypes   40

        The Working of these Archetypes   48

        The Dark Side   52

PART TWO: ANALYTIC INITIATION   57

Section One: Theory   61

Section Two: Experiences of Training   64

   Ordeal   64

   Disillusionment   67

   Integration   68

   Dreams   69

   Summary   72

Section Three: Archetypes   73

   Night Sea Journey and the Hero's Progress   73

   Fathers and Mothers   77

   Masculine and Feminine   78

   The Encounter with the Shadow   79

   The Archetype of the Self   81

PART THREE: CONCLUSIONS   83

   Initiation and Obedience   84

   Transformation   86

   Transformation and Death   88

   Inner/Outer: Self/Other   90

   Initiation and Mystery and Identity   90

   Identity and Individuation   92

Appendix I: A Second Theoretical Reflection on Training   95

Appendix II: A Zen Experience   99

Subject Index   105

ACKNOWLEDGMENTS

This manuscript has had a long history and so it would be impossible to name everyone I want to thank. From the first readers of its original form through the Jungian analysts who saw it as a thesis to the anonymous monk-reader who gave the conclusive suggestions for turning it into a book—all deserve my gratitude. Many friends have given comments, advice, suggestions. Dom Sebastian Moore wrote a preface I shall treasure, as I do his friendship. Many monastics, Jungian analysts in training, and seasoned analysts shared their experiences, which became part of the final version, as did the authors through the centuries on whose work I have drawn.

With regret for the anonymity of these acknowledgments, I can only repeat my thanks for many years of help, support, friendship, insight and example from all these people. It is certainly their book as much as mine.

PREFACE

Mary Wolff-Salin is doing that rare thing, asking the right question. She is doing an even rarer thing, asking *herself* the right question. Let me try to formulate the question.

There is the long and of course varied tradition of monastic formation, the education of mind and heart for a life that opens to the infinite but self-disclosing mystery. And there is what is available to us for the education of mind and heart *today* beyond the goals people normally set for themselves in our culture. How might we make the tradition of monastic conversion known to ourselves and to each other as moderns, as the persons we are, moved by what moves us, shaken by what shakes us?

The depth psychology of C. G. Jung is probably the best, at least most ample candidate for this translation. But the person undergoing this therapy, while open to the liminal and the counter-cultural, is still not in a position equivalent to someone living by monastic vows. Let me cite Eliot to describe such a person.

> Men's curiosity searches past and future
> And clings to that dimension. But to apprehend
> The point of intersection of the timeless
> With time, is an occupation for the saint—
> No occupation either, but something given
> And taken, in a lifetime's death in love
> Ardour and selflessness and self-surrender.

. . . .

> For most of us, this is the aim
> Never here to be realised.

We do not expect the analysand to cultivate ardor and selflessness and self-surrender. It is here that Mary makes her brilliant move. The equivalent, in contemporary psychological terms, of one who makes monastic profession is someone undergoing the rigors of *training* as an analyst, and Mary has no difficulty in matching the expectations and disappointments, the rage at being misunderstood, the perseverance through thick and thin, above all the exposure to the power of "superiors" with their limitations, with the conditions laid down in the Rule of St. Benedict. In this training, the modern psyche is exposed to appropriate trials.

Through this brilliant "conversion" from old to new, the tradition is saved from a literal reading that becomes moralistic, the monastic who works through the twelve degrees of humility going around with eyes on the ground beating the breast. And this monastic moralism can take far less caricatured forms than this, and still be moralistic and out of touch with the psyche and its joys and terrors, its ill-understood infrastructure, the real human stuff, what Mary at one point calls the *humanum*.

The Jungian trainee is becoming an expert in our fullest life, and thus reproducing the traditional monastic aim, to be wise and spreading of wisdom—a wisdom which the first monks could not have known, a wisdom, that is, able to speak to the painful problems with which our world is beset. When Dom Notker, our abbot primate, visits monasteries, he asks, "What do you do?" and when he gets the reply, "We keep the Rule," he expresses exasperation, saying, "You're supposed to be engaged in, and becoming wiser than, the culture you are living in. We don't want monastic mummies!" Mary's book is meeting this challenge in a creative, imaginative, and informed way. The devils with whom the ancient monks wrestled now have scientific names that connect them practically with our wounding and healing. There is a contemporary expertise for dealing with these energies, and a monastic formation today ignores such expertise at its peril, the peril precisely of mummification.

It has been wisely said that the demand made on us today, if we can face it, is to reenter the world of the primitive with our eyes open. This is what Mary's fine book is about. I believe that there is a new level of mutual recognition emerging between those who are experiencing this opening of the eyes to our infrastructure, to the deeper reaches of the human. This deep inner clarification of the humanum is generating a new Mariology, a new luminosity of the Song of Songs as celebrating the hieros gamos.

And it is, as Agatha the Anglican mystic says in that still important play of Eliot's *The Family Reunion,* "a common pursuit of liberation."

Sebastian Moore, O.S.B.
October 17, 2003

Jaffe
incarnating in the individual

INTRODUCTION

This book is born of the desire to explore the content of a long-term awareness and a long-term question—one shared, it would seem, by not a few reflective people today. It would seem that a necessary part of growing to maturity in all its stages has to do with passing through certain passages in life, even with going through certain experiences of a kind of testing one could call initiatory. But where are there, in today's cultures, authentic experiences of this nature? Is a boy's first driver's license, a girl's high school graduation, let alone a first experience of drink, drugs, sex such an initiation? Certainly these experiences initiate one into something—a certain kind of human experience, perhaps a certain kind of freedom. But this is not what initiation in earlier cultures was about. When anthropologists explain initiatory experiences—their stages, their effects—one sees their relevance for the society as a whole, for the individual involved, for the spiritual and psychological deepening and maturing of the human person. Such experiences are in a different category from the ones mentioned above, and one of the purposes of this book is to reflect on the nature of some modern parallels of these initiatory experiences. One would hope that this reflection would make it possible to see where, even today, young people—and older ones—can grow up without being deprived of the elements of true initiatory experience. This requires, however, that one reflect on what the elements of such experiences are or would need to be.

Long before there were any European- or African-Americans in the United States, the Native Americans had their own Vision Quest. This was not an easy process. Some contemporary groups are trying to resurrect or adapt aspects of this experience—for example in wilderness journeys. Still, in the very different culture we live in today, what can we learn from experiences like the Vision Quest?

A recent study of one form of initiation could perhaps give us some insight into this question. Placed not in the United States but in South Africa, it is a Jungian psychoanalyst and anthropologist's description of the formation of what we might call a Shaman or Medicine Person. Interestingly, the author finds important parallels between this process and the training of Jungian psychoanalysts—a subject that will be a major part of the reflection in this book.

Obviously the training of shamans is a different process than, say, a rite of passage for an adolescent male or female moving into adulthood. Nonetheless, looking at the picture in a somewhat magnified form will enable us to see important elements of the simpler processes as well. And, a little later in these pages, we will see what anthropology has to say about rites of passage in general so that we can find their basic ingredients for today.

It will be noticed that the initiatory experience Buermann discusses is prolonged. As a result it brings the person involved to new levels of experience. One might reflect, as one considers her account, that perhaps these are two important elements of any serious initiatory experience. The "change your self-concept in ten easy lessons," "learn to interpret dreams in ten easy lessons," and other such typically American quick fixes are precisely not what is being discussed here.

The illustrative study in question is called *Between two Worlds*.[1] The author, Vera Buermann, has lived a long time with the Xhosi. She begins with a description of the beginnings of a call to be a shaman, and one could reflect that in a Vision Quest a young Native American is trying precisely to find his own deep identity or call.

Among the Xhosi the call begins with a mysterious psychological illness born of the eruption of something new in the psyche. One could say that this is about a new awareness of what the Xhosi would call the call of the

---

[1] M. Vera Buermann, *Living in Two Worlds: Communication between a white healer and her black counterparts* (Chiron, Wilmette, Ill.: 1986).

Ancestors to serve them—or what a Jungian might call the demands of the Self[2] drawing one to live in a different way or embark on a different search. In her book, Buermann speaks of this psychological illness arising in the psyche and brooking no refusal. Or, in African terms, "*thwasa* . . . an emotional illness caused by the ancestors' call to serve them" is the beginning of the initiatory process that leads to becoming an *amaqqira* or shaman, and it can be seen in terms of the archetype of the Self and its demands. The initiatory process is carried on in an ongoing dialogue with the ancestors—or the Self—involving progressive degrees of purification and enlightenment. "He [the trainee] must undergo a gradual process of self-knowledge and maturation, and he must integrate previously unacknowledged and often previously unknown parts and aspects of his total personality."[3]

Buermann comments, "There are some startling similarities with the training of analytical psychologists." She continues, "The most important aim seems to be to strengthen the personality of the trainee and to help him to gear his life into one which will allow for 'the constant brooding of the ancestors' without becoming mentally disturbed." If one replaces the word "ancestors" with "archetypes" in this quotation, one can see the similarities of the two processes of training. She concludes her description of the process by saying:

> In summary, it can be postulated that through training, the deeper layers of the unconscious, which had been activated during *thwasa* and which had at first caused chaos and suffering, are now being gradually brought under control and are being integrated as meaningful manifestations of the human state. This is a process whereby the ego is confronted by the unconscious.[4]

[2] This difficult Jungian term is described in very different ways. For one example: "something . . . strange to us and yet so near, wholly ourselves and yet unknowable, a virtual centre of so mysterious a constitution that it can claim anything . . . the *self* . . . It might equally well be called the 'God within us.' The beginning of our whole psychic life seems to be inextricably rooted in this point, and all our highest and ultimate purposes seem to be striving towards it." C. G. Jung, *Collected Works*, R.F.C. Hull, trans., Bollingen Series XX (Princeton: Princeton University Press) 1953–1978. Henceforth referred to as "CW." Roman numerals refer to vol. nos.; Arabic to pars. VII, 398–99.

[3] Buermann, 69.

[4] Ibid., 75.

One fascinating thing about this quotation is its explanation of the reason for much of the experienced suffering. *Thwasa* is a psychological illness causing pain by the emergence of unconscious material but leading, in some cases, to therapeutic training which, because of its confrontations with the unconscious, causes further pain. One could say the main suffering of the process, however difficult its external hurdles, comes from within. It is about dealing with the call, with one's deeper self, and with domains within and beyond oneself that have previously escaped conscious awareness.

Each stage of the Xhosa process is marked by an appropriate ritual, and all ritual is seen as contact with the world of the ancestors. This is reminiscent of Turner's comments on the need for ritual[5] and our culture's impoverishment by its general absence today.

How much of all this is applicable to, say, adolescent initiation? All adolescents do not become healers but all have to deal with puberty and the upsurge of previously un-experienced material needing integration. Initiation is about ways in which this might be done.

As was said, most initiatory processes are not about becoming a shaman. They do, however, all involve a change in one's state of life or consciousness—and the passage through an experience of some kind of testing or liminality. A new kind of maturity is expected at the other end of the process. It may not be the level of integration of conscious and unconscious described by Buermann but it will certainly be concerned with maturation in some form.

It is time, here, to look at the anthropological understanding of initiation. But first, one final introductory note.

In my own experience, what prompted the project of this book was an increasing awareness of something that seemed strange. After years of experience of the initiatory stages of religious—and specifically monastic—life, I found myself exposed to a surprisingly similar process in Jungian psychoanalytic training. It was truly breath-taking to find, when one went deep enough, how many elements the two processes had in common. Superficially, one would expect similarities to be minimal. What could be more unlike a training that speaks of obedience and humility than a train-

---

[5] Victor Turner, *The Ritual Process: Structure and Anti-Structure* (Chicago: Aldine, 1969). Henceforth referred to as "Turner."

ing to be a psychoanalyst, to individuate? We shall see below just how superficial all elements of this judgment are. I would hope that by explaining these two training experiences in depth some sense of their deeper commonalities could be achieved—and, with it, some sense of what a contemporary initiatory experience might be. Few people enter monasteries or become analysts. But I would hope that not a few would recognize elements of other human experiences in what is said below.

I will, therefore, devote Part One to a discussion of monastic initiation seen in the form of a journal. Part Two will deal with Jungian training, and Part Three will try to draw some conclusions on human initiation in general.

PART ONE

MONASTIC INITIATION

―――――

SECTION ONE:
ANTHROPOLOGICAL REFLECTIONS ON INITIATION

For anthropology, what is initiation? What is the process for—or about? In much contemporary anthropological literature initiation is seen in terms of "rites of passage."

> The term initiation in the most general sense denotes a body of rites and oral teachings whose purpose is to produce a decisive alteration in the religious and social status of the person to be initiated. In philosophical terms, initiation is equivalent to a basic change in existential condition; the novice emerges from his ordeal endowed with a totally different being from that which he possessed before his initiation; he has become *another*.[1]

This quotation speaks for itself but deserves serious reflection. It is talking about a profound change in a human person who is very different before and after the initiatory process—different psychologically, affectively, socially, and otherwise. This change occurs precisely through the process of undergoing instruction, ordeals, and other constitutive elements of the initiatory experience.

According to anthropological studies, these rites of passage involve a three-part process: (1) separation from the group previously belonged to,

---

[1] Mircea Eliade, *Rites and Symbols of Initiation: the Mysteries of Birth and Rebirth*, Willard R. Trask, trans. (New York: Harper Torchbooks, Harper and Row) 1958, x.

(2) a period of liminality or "desert" where one belongs to no group and whose content will be discussed below, and (3) integration into the new community to which one will henceforth belong.

In order for this process to take place appropriately, the time of liminality includes certain standard phenomena. There is normally an ordeal, even a torture of some kind, in which—in the case of boys—a kind of manhood or fortitude is demonstrated. But the experience may also be a kind of symbolic death. There is also the experience of being subject, obedient, to the "elders" who represent the tradition of the tribe and who pass on its mysteries. There are, of course, as many types of initiation as there are cultures. Men and women, Africans and Native Americans are not initiated in the same way. It becomes necessary, then, to see what models are appropriate for the present study. I suggest, however, that in almost all cases five elements form part of this liminal stage: (1) an ordeal, (2) obedience to the elders who represent the collectivity, (3) the receiving of the tradition passed on by these elders, (4) a relationship with a teacher or spiritual guide, and (5) a connection with a sacred source.

A tradition may be passed on in various ways. A body of myths and stories is one classical way. An apprenticeship to a guru of some kind is another. A lonely "vision quest" is still another that frequently follows the first two.

It is worth pointing out that the "torture" element that I judge not to be an essential part of the process (see Part Two) has, nonetheless, been seen by more than one "initiator" as essential. It seems to be the accepted wisdom in many traditions that one cannot fully become who one is without going through a serious amount of suffering. Why would this be so? The suffering is not always intentionally inflicted. It is simply part of the process.

In order to flesh out more thoroughly some rudiments of scholarly thought on the subject, we cannot do better than to follow some reflections of Victor Turner in his, now classical *The Ritual Process*, referred to above. In one of his first studies there, Turner remarks that the couple undergoing this specific process are naked except for narrow waist-cloths: "This is said to represent the fact that they are at once like infants and corpses."[2] One element of the "betwixt and between" nature of initiation

---

[2] Turner, 31.

is that the initiand is no longer what he/she was and is not yet what he/she is to become. During this middle stage previous identity is swept away and so one is really like an infant or corpse.

In a detailed discussion of rites of passage Turner goes on:

> This theme [liminality and community] is in the first place represented by the nature and characteristics of what Arnold van Gennep (1960) has called "the liminal phase" of *rites de passage*. Van Gennep himself defined *rites de passage* as "rites which accompany every change of place, state, social position and age." To point up the contrast between "state" and "transition," I employ "state" to include all his other terms. . . . Van Gennep has shown that all rites of passage or "transition" are marked by three phases: separation, margin (or *limen,* signifying "threshhold" in Latin), and aggregation. The first phase (of separation) comprises symbolic behavior signifying the detachment of the individual or group either from an earlier fixed point in the social structure, from a set of cultural conditions (a "state"), or from both. During the intervening "liminal" period, the characteristics of the ritual subject (the "passenger") are ambiguous; he passes through a cultural realm that has few or none of the attributes of the past or coming state. In the third phase (reaggregation or reincorporation), the passage is consummated. The ritual subject, individual or corporate, is in a relatively stable state once more and, by virtue of this, has rights and obligations vis-à-vis others of a clearly defined and "structural" type; he is expected to behave in accordance with certain customary norms and ethical standards binding on incumbents of social position in a system of such positions.[3]

When we speak of the process of initiation, then, we are speaking most specifically of the liminal phase between the beginning and end of the process. This fact explains some of the elements of liminality listed above. Turner adds, "Liminality is frequently likened to death, to being in the womb, to invisibility, to darkness, to bisexuality, to the wilderness, and to an eclipse of the sun or moon."[4] Liminal entities, he continues, are represented as possessing nothing, showing passive or humble behavior, obeying their instructors implicitly, and accepting arbitrary punishment

[3] Ibid., 94–95.
[4] Idem.

without complaints. We shall be speaking below of the applicability of some of these traits to initiation in our contemporary culture.

Speaking of the initiation of a chief-to-be, Turner mentions a custom by which the chief is roundly insulted by the one conducting the ceremony. Anyone else who feels that he (or she?) has been wronged by the chief-to-be may also speak. There may be no future resentment for any of this, for the chief must go into his position from this place of humility that will, hopefully, enable him to live well in community with his tribe.

> This community is the repository of the whole gamut of the culture's values, norms, attitudes, sentiments and relationships. Its representatives in the specific rites—and these may vary from ritual to ritual—represent the generic authority of tradition. In tribal societies, too, speech is not merely communication but also power and wisdom. The wisdom (*mana*) that is imparted in sacred liminality is not just an aggregation of words and sentences; it has ontological value, it refashions the very being of the neophyte.[5]

Coming, as we do, out of a culture that values individuality (or individualism!) more than community and a kind of adolescent kill-the-father attitude over any notion of respect for authority (now seen as some sort of lack of personal freedom), we place ourselves in a position which renders any classical form of initiation difficult at best. Once again, reflecting on these points is one of the purposes of these pages. Clearly the United States is not Africa, and what we do we do as who we are. The question is: are there valid forms of initiation in our culture that serve similar ends to these others, and, if so, how do they work?

Turner himself comments, "Nowhere has this institutionalization of liminality been more clearly marked and defined than in the monastic and mendicant states in the great world religions."[6] In the sense of a life marginal to the contemporary culture and its values, this is surely so. On the other hand, within these life-forms themselves, there is also the phenomenon of initiation as Part One and also the last appendix will show. As we enter into two contemporary forms of initiatory processes perhaps some of the above elements of initiation will begin to make more sense. And

[5] Ibid., 103.
[6] Ibid., 107.

perhaps the ones that need to be questioned for us today will reveal what forms they might take instead. In any case, one can only gain by reflection on such experience.

This very preliminary sketch is meant to give just a few basic lines of the concept of initiation. It is illustrated in much greater depth and more concretely in the pages that follow, but perhaps the structure with which Turner has supplied us will enable better reflection on the contemporary phenomena.

Section Two: A Monastic Journal

Introduction

As was said above, this journal is fictitious, but rather in the way that a case study is fictitious. It combines the experiences of many people into a single story. What is important in this story is the process involved, the gradual development of a human person over a period of several years, so that she ends this period in a very different "space" from the one where she began it. One can note various elements that played on or in her psyche as time passed. Can one see them causally? Yes and no, I believe. Yes, in a monastic setting the teaching of the elders, the stories of the tradition, repeated in Scripture, liturgy, the tradition, teaching, the steady perseverance through the ordeals of the life, the deepening relationship with God—all these work on the soul, psyche, body of the person involved and this causes change. But it is rare indeed that one can assign any precise causality, or, for that matter, even define a change with any real clarity. Behavior shows, attitudes and feelings may show. But what happened in a person's depths remains mystery.

With all this said, then, the journal can speak for itself. A kind of interdisciplinary reflection on the experience described will follow.

Journal

February 1

So here I am at last—where I never expected to be; where I have always been and still am half afraid to be. Certainly none of my friends ever expected to see me in a monastery—nor do they expect me to stay. A thirty-five-year-old with a marriage and a psychology degree and practice behind her—with what seems to them much too much worldly sophistication for such a choice—hardly seems an appropriate candidate for such a life. And yet, here I am. There will be hard moments, I know . . . beginning now. Others here come from very different backgrounds from mine, notably as regards study. Will we understand each other?

And I? Will I possibly be able to persevere in a life so utterly other from anything I have known? And yet, in coming here I followed my heart, my deepest desire—with which all my superficial desires conflict—the deepest space within me and its longing. I have never so far been wrong when I have done this, even in the face of warnings, if I listened seriously. I hope (and half hope not) that may be true of this choice as well.

The arrival was intimidating—the opening of the huge cloister doors, that so rarely are opened, to admit me; the greeting by the entire community with its formal, but astonishingly welcoming, kiss of peace; and then immediately the first Vespers of tomorrow's feast, the Purification. Well, it's done. I'm inside these walls—so forbidding from outside. We'll see how it goes.

February 2

I got wax on my coat at the procession of candles for the feast and went upstairs to the habit sister to get it removed. She smiled at me and said, "If God wills this, he will make it easy. You'll see." Well, yes. We will indeed see.

February 10

It has been a hard week. After braving all the opposition to come into a place of silence where I could hear the voice of God, "the whisper of a gentle breeze," I hear *nothing*. Only a resounding silence. Nothing in the Psalms we chant daily speaks to me; nothing in the readings at meals or elsewhere. I hope this won't go on long.

February 18

I just reread the last entry. It *is* going on. Maybe two weeks doesn't seem long, but in this setting and with these feelings it seems an eternity. If things don't change, can I go on?

February 28

I've been here a month, and the going is still very rough. The novice mistress is away convalescing and I don't tell the abbess much about how I feel, so I'm alone with the weight of this empty silence.

Still, I must admit that somewhere deep inside some things begin to speak to me—the simplicity of the Psalms we say at the Little Hours: "You have gathered my tears into your jar"; the quiet rhythm of the day with its sense of freedom and space; the beauty of the hills from my cell window. It is like a sense of peace hidden deep under the pain. But the pain is stronger—and the weight of the silence.

March 1

A sudden cold chill hit me this morning. Can I do this? Can I go on? What if it is always like this—dead? Empty silence? Dead inside?

I just don't know. I'll have to wait and see. Probably I should talk to someone about it—or write Father Gregory. But I chill inside at the thought. This could very well be a sign of non-vocation, couldn't it? If I decide, OK, but how will I feel if someone else—someone with authority—says it to me? Right now the thought is too much. I don't want to talk about it.

March 8

The novice mistress returned from her rest time. I like her very much. She is only a few years older than I and very unassuming but she really lives this life. She saw all six of us individually yesterday for an hour. I told her how I was feeling and she answered, "All that matters is to be yourself as you are and to live face to face with God." It sounds simple but her saying it brought peace. Though it is hard, too.

There is another level of peace, though, from having told her—having been myself at my negative worst and receiving her calm response, "Be yourself." The notion that I can be myself as I am and have that be the best way to be contemplative is healing. Psychologically I know this kind of thing, but it is very different to be told it here. Benedict's exhortations to be open about one's worst thoughts to a spiritual father or mother begin to make a new kind of sense in this situation. I hope I will have the courage to remember this and continue it.

March 20

I am concerned about Teresa—a postulant who arrived just about when I did. She stands in choir with her hands so tightly clasped that the knuckles show white. (And I won't even mention her theories about monasticism: "It is not monastic to wash underclothes daily," for example!)

Why does she annoy me as much as she does? (She told the novice mistress I won't even meet her eyes.) Maybe I fear that there might be a streak of that rigidity and pietism in me?? Well, I know I can be rigid, but some kinds of piety turn my stomach. Why? The novice mistress commented, "Would it bother you if it were happening in another monastery far from here?" Then why does it bother me here?

But I truly worry about her tenseness.

While I'm on about tension, the raucous croaking of my neighbor in choir, Agatha, continues to drive me crazy. Why can't she pipe down? She certainly can't sing. And eight offices a day beside her really mount up. Am I going to spend the rest of my monastic life with that raucous off-tune croaking in my ear for several hours a day? It almost ruins the Office for me.

A priest here to give the community a weekend retreat was scandalized when I said that to him. He lectured me about the beauty and nobility of the vocation and asked how one could get so lost in petty details as this. He doesn't live them! Our life is made of these "details." Besides, this "pay no attention to your feelings" bit is the worst side of Catholicism. (Some very unconscious Catholicism.) But when one does attend to them—ouch!

I am torn between my growing love of the life and its beauty—and of the people here whom I increasingly love—and my exasperation with things like this Office problem. Is it insoluble? How should it be solved? I'd like them to ask her to quiet down, but when they do the effects only last a few days. One can't very well make a good voice a prerequisite for a monastic vocation! Can one say to someone, "*Always* just mouth the words: give no voice"? Then she suffers. This way, we suffer—or I do. Is this a life that just by its intrinsic nature inflicts suffering? Does the fact of community mean the omnipresence of suffering? There is joy, too, from friendships and beauty and so many things. But this exasperation is very painful and strong. Amazing how a tiny thing can be like a speck in one's eye and take all one's attention.

April 1

April Fool's Day. And almost the beginning of Holy Week. This Lent has been hard and depressing. Fasting, many nights without recreation, exhortations to penance in the readings we hear, something about the whole mood. Very heavy. That's not supposed to be Benedictine: we "look forward to holy Easter . . . with joy." I don't feel joy. I want this long cold winter to be over—four layers of sweaters! This building resists the little heat they put on.

Why am I so depressed? Well, I suppose hunger, cold and silence will do it. I hope this passes. . . . Every time it recurs I say to myself again, do this for the rest of my life?

Easter

It passed all right! The depth and beauty of the Holy Week services—and life—are beyond talking about. Palm Sunday doesn't move me much. But Holy Thursday really did. The Mandatum where the abbess washed—and kissed—the novices' feet and did it as if she meant it. I really do love her, though occasionally I get exasperated with her—and she with me—and sparks fly. But she has depth . . . and she suffered a lot as a young nun, and later as well. It mellows a person.

The liturgy brought the Last Supper and the meaning of the Eucharist home to me as never before. Poignant. And then the stripped, severe reenactment of Good Friday. I went out to walk in the garden for a lot of the time between noon and 3:00 p.m. when the crucifixion ordeal was over for Christ. And what haunted me during that time, and since, were Christ's words to the thief dying beside him: "*Today* you will be with me in Paradise." Today. Is that what gave him the courage and serenity to endure? Is that our promise as well? Is it a promise for me? Is today now? I feel as if it could be. Paradise here, and we don't know it. My Irish monk friend speaks of "thin" times, when the veil between time and eternity is "thin," almost gone.

And then the long celebration of the Easter Vigil Saturday night—fire blessed in the darkness, candle flames passed from person to person until the whole church is lit up, the Exultet chant—beautifully done. ("O happy fault, . . . Most blessed of all nights, . . .") And after all was over, the procession to the statue of Mary in the cloister to sing, "Rejoice . . . for your Son is risen as he said." I could feel that joy as if the inner winter, like the outer, were over as the buds begin to burgeon on the trees.

May 1

I haven't written for a long time. It has been such a quiet happy time. The buds are bursting into flower; the birds are singing—and mating; a new little calf was born in the barn; and we go on long walks at recreation. Eastertide is a real, long gift.

More and more I think I might be staying. There's a deep peace growing beneath the surface storms—a peace I've not known before. I begin to feel like a fish in the right kind of water—as if I'd never found that "right kind" before. Not that some things don't annoy me. Not that there aren't things I'd hope to see changed. But still . . . .

On the other hand, it is increasingly borne in upon me that a few of the nuns—notably some older ones—really disapprove of me. Teresa left last week after what amounts to a breakdown. As I was reading the bulletin board outside the community room, I heard one elderly nun inside say to another, "She was very dear," and the other responded, "What do you expect—being a postulant together with a doctor in psychology?"

So much for what they think of me! Will many of them vote against my admission to vows? Who knows? It's still far away. On the other hand, it is getting to be time to think about requesting the habit of a novice, "Clothing," as they call it.

May 15

I really want to keep on journaling—at least weekly or fortnightly. It makes me more conscious of where I am internally and what is going on.

Increasingly I feel at peace with this life. And I am going to request Clothing as a novice. Who knows if I'll make it to Profession? But I do feel ready for this next step. I suppose June is the moment to ask—two months before the Clothing would take place. But the novice mistress knows how I feel, doubts and all, and is encouraging.

June 1

Well, I did it! I spoke to the abbess and prioress about becoming a novice. It feels much more definitive, now that I've made that commitment. I did tell them that I didn't know if I'd ever feel ready to make Profession—vows that are binding for ever. But they just said, "One step at a time. That's what a novitiate is for."

Father Mark was over yesterday, and we had a long walk in the garden. I told him all this and he said, "Nobody knows if he—or she—will go on at this stage. Some people just think they do."

I also told him some of my problems with the community—their age and a certain heaviness, unwillingness to think about change. He said, "Well, don't the young people get a chance to talk together about this?"

I was amazed—and reassured—amazed because, to listen to the gossip, one would think he'd never allow that in his monastery. And apparently the gossip is totally false. Reassured because there is strength in such "connecting."

June 8

I am feeling really socked in the stomach. My friend Cecile is a nun in a monastery with real abuses. She wrote a whole long letter about nothing changing. I fear she'll leave and that really worries me: she had to fight so long and hard to get there.

June 15

Well, I've cooled down a bit since the last entry—though only a bit. None of that stuff I wrote about is OK but . . . it is their issue and it is they who have to get on their feet and refuse to live in that way.

And if the majority can't?

Then those who see must live their own lives as they need to—hard, but true.

June 22

A long meeting with the abbess about the Clothing. It seems that I am accepted and the date will probably be August 15—or September 8. It's not clear yet. I want the Gospel of the Annunciation. Will that be possible? We'll see.

June 29

Every Wednesday at Vespers I wait for Psalm 137. I wish we sang it—or had a soloist sing it—with the Oriental melody I first heard. I will never forget Father Gregory, the day I first went to his monastery, singing it for Julia and me with guitar in their little chapel, "If I forget you, Jerusalem, ... Let my tongue cling to the roof of my mouth, . . ."

All the longing of the Hebrews was in it—harps hung on poplars in Babylon: "How could we sing the Lord's song in a foreign land?" And then, "If I forget you, Jerusalem . . ."

Jerusalem, the city of peace. I felt so deeply on alien soil, then—so far from the "city of peace." I guess for me that has always been what the monastery represented—the place of peace, longed for from alien soil— even when I fought the longing and thought the price too high to pay.

One soon learns, inside, that there is peace and peace. A monastic setting doesn't guarantee peace. Inside as well as out there are conflicts, disagreements, annoyances. But the life is structured to further inner peace if one is strong enough to seek the real monastery, the real Jerusalem, within.

It is a hard lesson for me to learn. I always want external peace and harmony. But paradise is lost, as Milton said. It is foolish to be unrealistic.

Still, Merton writes about monastic life as a recovery of the lost paradise.[1] Will it really become that? How? I wonder . . . .

Some of the old nuns—even some of the younger ones—have found their peace. One sees it in their faces, even in their walk and movement. Meanwhile, "Jerusalem" recurs in psalm after psalm and reading after reading—a central symbol and one that speaks deeply to me.

July 1

A letter from Cecile—she is leaving her monastery. She expects to transfer to another, ultimately, but she needs time to heal first. She says several others are considering similar moves. I feel the same rage, frustration, helplessness as before. It is all very distressing. And now I wish I could see Cecile. These are the moments when cloister is really hard.

July 6

The latest pre-postulant strikes me as having major sexual problems. She can't talk to someone without getting so close as to invade their personal space in a very seductive way. I was told to take her upstairs to do Yoga during the siesta hour in the hope that it would be a calming influence, but she manages to make even that a sexual experience. A few days ago I heard the novice mistress—who is the calmest and gentlest person alive—snap at her, "Stop touching me." I'd make a serious bet that her past, despite her youth, includes some experiences people here don't even imagine, and I wouldn't be surprised to learn that she had been on the streets.

How did someone like that get in? (And what is she seeking?) One wonders who did the screening. But I wouldn't give her another month here at the rate things are going.

It's funny about sex. The standard wisdom is that celibacy is much harder for people who have been sexually active. And I've at least two very good friends here who weren't before entering but who consider themselves over-sexed, because they are easily aroused—one at prayer, one in relationships or by beauty or by lots of things. Why on earth call that *over*-sexed?

Still, I am struck by how little I have had to struggle on that front. Is it partly the pain of a short marriage ending in such a traumatic accident? Working through that therapeutically is what got me into psychology

---

[1] See Thomas Merton, *The Waters of Siloe* (San Diego: A Harvest/HBJ Book, Harcourt, Brace, Jovanovich, 1949) 37–49. Henceforth referred to as *Siloe*.

studies. If John had lived, I'd have been a million miles from here. Still, that pain and that death—mine as well as his—have brought me to a place I'd never have thought to be, internally as well as externally.

Wherever he is, I'm sure he knows and understands.

July 20

I went over the Clothing ceremonial with the abbess. They're letting me choose my own texts and music by putting the ceremony on the eve of the Assumption. There is nothing in the wording of the ceremony that I find problematical, as I feared I might, given my questions about Profession. It looks very simple, sober, sane, honest.

August 1

I am going into retreat for Clothing. They gave me two weeks. I never expected to see this day—to find myself facing the prospect of the Habit and all it signifies. It isn't something little and trivial, as I've heard some active Sisters—and some nuns!—say. It symbolizes a whole way of life. It is like a movable cloister one carries around, a way of being "hidden in God's face" even while visible. I'm amazed that I can see all this positively, amazed that I could possibly want it. (Though I'm glad we now, like the monks, have the option of getting out of it on occasion. That feels important. But the issue now is what it means to wear it.)

August 14

Well, the day is over. It has been such an incredible experience of depth and happiness that I don't want to go to bed and have it end.

It began with the Chapter. I expected to feel nothing, though I rather gulped as I put on my "secular clothes" for the last time.

When I got to the Chapter Room, the whole community was there. The abbess asked the ritual question: "What do you ask?" and, as I knelt down in the middle of all those people and said, "The mercy of God and to share your monastic life," I suddenly meant it with every fiber of my being. *This* life with *these* people—the ones I love and the ones I love less—in *this* monastery. And I do mean for ever. It was lucky that was the last thing I had to say. I couldn't have uttered another word. When the abbess and novice mistress put the habit on me and embraced me, my eyes overflowed and I couldn't speak.

Father Gregory said Mass. The homily was about Mary, for the Assumption, but it was also about me. I was again moved almost beyond bearing as he spoke of the long road that led to this place. I know now that I will make Profession. This is what I have wanted all my life without knowing it. Now I know.

After Mass we—the abbess, novitiate, Father Gregory and I—went to the parlor for some wine and cheese. Afterwards he commented to me, "I kept the conversation going, because I could see that you couldn't." How like him to know that!

People say I look as natural in the habit as if I'd been born in it. And that's how it feels.

Christmas Day

It's been a long time with no journaling. "Happy countries have no history." Midnight Mass was an incredible experience. All through Advent one waits, prepares, hopes—and thinks: "How can I ever be ready" for something like Incarnation. God becoming a baby: it's impossible. And preparation seems impossible: my house is too small. The world is too small.

And then, mysteriously, the whole thing is taken to a different level: that incredible opening chant: *Dominus dixit ad me, Filius meus es tu. Ego hodie genui te* ("The Lord said to me, you are my son. Today I have begotten you"). *Hodie.* Today eternity comes into time. One almost experiences it.

The whole of this life would be worth it to come to such experiences of meaning. When the Christmas glow is over, may I remember that!

February 1

It has been six months and only one entry. I didn't need to write, or want to. The joy of the Clothing lasted for months, followed by the beauty of Advent and Christmas. The cold is always something of a problem, but I've learned how to dress. The workshop on the Rule that I was sent out to stirred up a few things. Male and female novices and juniors from various places and some excellent speakers. I always get perturbed about some of this obedience stuff. It's so easy to misuse on either end—blind, childish dependence and irresponsibility on the one hand and authoritarianism on the other. Still, I learned some interesting things, made friends with some people from other monasteries, and enjoyed the experience.

February 20

We had a heavy duty liturgy meeting. I knew the community was very deeply divided: keep Office and Mass in Latin or change to the vernacular.

Latin has the beautiful centuries-old chants, rich with tradition and depth of meaning and a music so beautiful that Bach pales in comparison. It is a music that is also psychologically creative of prayer. Even after a year, all this has seeped deeply into my being: it feels like *the* monastic culture and tradition, bringing out the full significance of each season and feast.

But the vernacular is our language. The Psalms bring one up short in a very different way in one's own language—and the same is true for more modern readings. It is like being brought totally back into the human world of passion and pain, hour by hour suffering at injustice and mistreatment, feeling betrayal, hatred, joy, love, trust. All this is newly experienced in a modern language.

Need we choose? Many say, "No hodge-podges."

It was a hard meeting. I knew the "progressives" would ask the novices' views to strengthen their case. I also knew it was not politic to give my views. But I spoke in favor of the vernacular with a plea to retain the most beautiful chants nonetheless. And after the meeting I found myself counting the votes I had probably lost toward acceptance for Profession. I need two-thirds of the Chapter: will I still get it?

But I can't live in fear. I have to be who I am. A young monk friend just accepted for Solemn Vows said at a meeting of our two communities, "I have lived my whole formation time in fear."

I just *won't* do that. And yet—what if they send me away? I love this place and its spirit: the loss would be well-nigh unbearable.

It's a hard place to be in, but, as Luther said, "Here I stand. I can't do anything else." If one won't stand up and be counted, what kind of life will one turn one's existence into?

March 20

It is halfway through my second Lent. It's less depressing this year. I wonder why. Maybe I've got into the Lenten "space" better—the desire for more silence and simplicity and reflection so that I can enter with deeper understanding—no, experience—into the mystery, death/resurrection. After all, how much one dies all the time! I was shocked when a lovely warm-hearted monk-friend, preaching the other day, said, "God will ask of us, as of Abraham, what we love most."

My first reaction was anger: "What horrid god-image is that?" But then I reflected: couples married forty or fifty years separated by death; old people moving out of a life-time house; mothers losing children—

whether literally to illness or simply because the child moves in a different direction, and on and on. "He's right," I thought, "hard but true." We do have to learn to come to terms with death—all kinds of death. And who knows what will arise in its place? I want to finish Lent seriously this year in that light.

May 8

I've been doing a lot of thinking about poverty. I get very concerned about the size of this building (it was built for twice the number of nuns); the cost of heating it; the excellence of the cooking; and, above all, the sort of out-of-touchness I sometimes feel with suffering outside. They were reading in the refectory a letter from the Brazilian bishops, "I have heard the cry of my people." I could hardly swallow my soup. Later I asked the novice mistress why people seemed so impervious: little was even said about it at recreation. She answered, "Enough years in the cloister, and some of this can get to seem pretty remote, not that it should."

I really don't want that to happen to me.

May 30

I was working in the novitiate library today and saw a paper on the desk. It was a conference given after the death of the founding abbess by her successor. It said something like: "There shouldn't be much to say about the life of a Benedictine nun when she dies—her life should be so at one with the liturgy, so lost in this greater whole."

In a way that sounds terrible—where is the person's individuality? But in a way it sounds wonderful—to be lost in the deepest mysteries, meaning, transformation of human experience. That is not to be lost: it is to be most deeply oneself, paradoxically. What the women here, some of them, seem to be. The "Our Father" text is painted across the choir stalls. A Sister-visitor asked me, "Do you here have special devotion to the Our Father?" I tried to say that the whole point here is that there are no "special devotions"—that the issue is a return to absolute fundamentals. It's very hard to express.

June 15

A good friend who works in the infirmary just told me about an experience that really brought her up short. She has several incontinent old nuns, and one or two really difficult ones up there and gets very tired. She was wheeling one along, complaining and fussing. Suddenly she thought,

"If I just let go of the wheelchair, it will roll down the ramp and crash and I'll have some peace." A moment later she thought, aghast, "I'm a potential murderer."

We talked a long time about the experience—about how crucial it is never to forget our deep kinship with the people in the prisons and the combat zone. Not "There but for the grace of God go I," but "There go I." The cloister walls buffer us from a lot of difficulties—though they close us in with a lot more. But if we forget the kinship—even that identity in humanness—we're sunk and can live a totally fake life.

July 16

An interesting sentence from Han de Wit's *Contemplative Psychology.* "We could regard the transformation of the states [of being or mind] on the contemplative way as an increasing capacity to remain open to the energy and fullness of the basic ground of reality."[2]

In carefully secular language, I suppose that *is* what it's all about—increasing consciousness of the Ground of one's being, increasing awareness of that other Dimension we so often miss. That really is what the life and all its practices are for.

De Wit says the two levels of development are this one and compassion (where compassion is imperfect, so is spiritual development. He comes from a Buddhist as much as a Christian perspective.) That makes sense. Maybe it's why I get a smidgeon less irritated with Agatha *et al* than a year ago. (Though my hair still stands on end when there is discussion of Teresa returning.) Fortunately all this is not something one does by personal effort. It happens month by month, year by year—and then one day one notices that it has happened.

August 14

Anniversary of my Clothing. It seems longer—in the sense that I feel as if I'd been here for years. It feels natural to be here. (Maybe that's why people said that the minute I was clothed I looked as if I had always worn the Habit. Are there "naturals" for this kind of life?)

And yet . . . there are moments when I wonder: have I gotten myself into a dead end, an *impasse*? Will the language of liturgy never change out

[2] Han F. De Wit, *Contemplative Psychology,* M. L. Baird, trans. (Pittsburgh: Duquesne University Press, 1991) 57.

of Latin, and will I be angry if it doesn't? Will the heavy burden of outdated customs ever change? Will it be OK for me to live here if nothing changes? Will it be suffocating, or have I found enough of my inner way to inner freedom? Perhaps above all, will the refusal to change out-dated customs come to mean that there will no longer be the time for prolonged quiet prayer and reflection? This could be very serious for me, and I need to face how deeply this question worries me and think it through. I want this life—and partly do not want it. We'll have to see what the next year shows.

September 8

A beautiful Marian feast. I love the music of the Eastern chant we used.

But what really knocked me over at Mass was some words I hear every single day that suddenly came alive—the words around the Our Father that ask for peace in the world, freedom from anxiety, joyful hope for the future and then ask for the peace and unity of Christ's kingdom where He lives—here and now for us. It is, again, the Celtic notion of "thin" places and times—Christ living in an eternal kingdom of peace and unity and that being present here and now if we could break through into it—or rather, it to us. We've trivialized all this Celtic thought into the idea that the Irish believe that fairies are present, and then we have parades with leprechauns—while the real idea behind the whole thing is the presence of other worlds behind or under or beside this one—worlds to which we are blind. I wonder why?

October 1

Sister Agatha's Profession. Her petition in Chapter to be accepted was really touching. She basically said she had come here old because she wanted to give her last years to God and she was grateful to have been so lovingly received.

I wish her the very best. Her voice at Office still annoys me a lot, but it doesn't drive me quite as crazy as it used to. I suppose I lose myself more in the rhythm of the chant and the movement of the Office. It becomes a sort of mantric process—even almost a dance—that becomes its own specific form of prayer. And if some of it is ugly, OK. The chantress singing one note sharp to keep the choir's tone up is just as bad as Agatha.

November 2

I have been reading William of St. Thierry. He says, of knowing God, "It is the kind of knowledge one has of a friend . . . that is direct and incommunicable, a knowledge of the heart that is too complex, too deep, to be formulated in concepts or words, but that is nonetheless true."[3]

How perfectly said! This is something one just can't explain to people who don't know it. "What ARE you doing, wasting your life in a place like this? You're doing nothing of any significance—no husband, no children, no work, no service" and on and on. And, of course, the snide remarks about sexual frustration in celibacy. There *is* no answer. Either you understand or you don't. What William of St. Thierry is talking about is the very heart of this life—a growing relationship that, like any relationship, cannot really be described.

November 27

This is the last visiting day before Advent. And the last journal must have been prophetic. A visit from Aunt Winifred—Protestant branch of the family and comments all too predictable. "Such a waste, my dear, you being locked up in a place like this . . . . Still, one understands, of course, after dear John's death. Such a tragedy."

I had to bite back my anger. (And maybe I shouldn't have.) She'd never understand that my being here and John's death are not causally connected.

Well, they are. If he were alive, where would I be now? Not here, certainly. But my anguish over his death was one thing; the growing pull to come here—and my resistance—was another: two different wave-lengths.

Can it be? Since both went very deep? Do they meet on the unconscious level? Is it all about love—*eros*—longing? I suppose. Augustine would say so: "My love is my weight." (In the sense that God is the magnet.)

Oh, bother the whole thing! I'm here. I'm staying (I hope!) And who cares about family gossip?

November 30

I've been having rather a bad cough. Now the novice mistress says she thinks I had better see a doctor. I hate the thought, but the appointment is made for tomorrow.

December 4

Bad news. The doctor called us back with the lab results, and it appears that not only do I have incipient tuberculosis, but he said all sorts of

---

[3] William of St. Thierry quoted in Edward Sellner, *Soul-Making: the Telling of a Spiritual Journey* (Mystic, Conn.: Twenty-Third, 1991) 93.

things about the climate here being bad for me, the almost unheatable building, etc., etc.—very nervous-making, but I told him this was important to me and I was going to stay.

December 6

My world just fell apart. The abbess called me this morning and said that they could not take the responsibility to admit me to vows in light of everything the doctor said. She said I could stay for another month or even two, since the cold has not hit yet this year, and they would do all they could to "nurse me back to health," but that my health really did not allow me to make monastic profession.

I feel absolutely desperate. It has taken me so long to be sure this is really my "way" and now I *am* really sure. Now that I know this is really what I want with the whole of my being, how can I possibly have to go? God *can't* be doing this! I'm sure it is all a bad dream, and soon I'll wake up.

December 9

The bad dream is continuing all too badly. I called the doctor's office to ask if there was any possibility of mis-diagnosis or any possibility that he would withdraw his recommendation that I could not live here. "No" to both.

God, what are You doing? And WHY? It makes a nonsense out of my whole life. It seems as if there has been a golden thread drawing me here, leading in this direction, half unknown to me for the whole of my life. How can You possibly let it all blow up now? WHY?

December 11

Things get worse and worse. I find myself getting angry at God and tempted to blasphemy. Is God simply the Great Torturer? *Is* there a God? I'm afraid I always think there is, but what do we know about the nature of such a Being? What makes us think God is good? Maybe just the contrary! Sometimes it feels a sheer nonsense to think that God guides our lives—let alone for the good. I can't read. I can't pray. I can't find any peace. And I'm sure this is not the way to get better physically—not that I care any more. If people still die of this, death might be welcome.

December 20

All the beauty of the Advent season is lost on me. I can't wait for Christmas or feel any joy or longing. I only feel as if my world has come to an end. People say to me, "You can live the monastic spirit anywhere"—so easy to say out of the safety of the enclosure! *They* don't live in the world I left two + years ago with its noise, its pressure, its crazy values. I'm sure some saints can live inner silence anywhere. I'm not a saint. I need this stillness, the liturgy and the office, this kind of life. And maybe, if God is vicious, that is why I am losing them.

December 24

Do I have any faith any more? This has always been one of the most beautiful days of the year for me, and now it is straw. The chants mean nothing; the liturgy means nothing; when people preach about the love of God coming to us as a child, I think, "Oh, yeah?" The thought of suicide does indeed recur, but I suppose I don't want to court damnation. Though I can imagine a moment of such desperation that I'd be past thinking of that . . . I've felt that way at moments.

Actually, I suppose this is a culmination of many earlier moments of doubt. I remember my despair at the time of the accident. But somehow, this is the worst so far—maybe because it is indeed a culmination.

December 25

The novice mistress took me for a long walk today. I say "Took me" deliberately: I would just have stayed in my cell, looking at the walls. Her ability just to be with my pain was . . . not healing. Nothing can be healing. But it helped. I feel less alone. But I'll lose her as well when I leave. The abbess, too, is being very loving—and that only makes things worse. And this is Christmas! I haven't even been able to get myself to open gifts my family sent. I don't want to do anything, say anything, even move.

December 28

I took a "Desert Day" today and went down to the very edge of the property and just sat. I didn't pray. I just sat on a rock near the woods. Somewhere deep inside I began to feel that who I am is who I am. My external circumstances are not going to change that, unless I let them. I can choose my circumstances, to some degree. I can decide how I want to live. That brought some tiny beginning of peace. Father Gregory will be here tomorrow. Will that help?

December 30

Talking with Father Gregory did help a bit. He is very strong, and I felt as if I "caught" some of that strength. He kept saying things much like my reflections on the rock: no one can change your inner options unless you do. But he also went to the abbess and asked for a prolongation of my time here. He said it very firmly; so she agreed. It's better. I don't feel ready to leave.

January 15

Oddly, I've been feeling internally stronger. I still rage internally when someone says something pious like, "Well, all we want is God's Will, isn't it?" Not me, I don't! Not this one! Besides, how do we know what is God's Will? I finally said to someone in rage, "Was the Vietnam War God's Will just because it happened?" She didn't try to answer.

All this makes one rethink everything—theology, God-image, simplistic ways of seeing things, simplistic answers. None of that holds. I've often asked myself lately, "Have I still faith?" For some time I thought not. Conceptually it certainly seems not. But I still want to go to Communion; so I suppose that says something about the non-conceptual level. Maybe one has to spend the whole of one's life reformulating what faith one has. Or rather, maybe formulations matter less and less, but that isn't true either. Some things one has to believe or one isn't Christian. There's a basic honesty involved in facing that. Can I be Christian if I doubt that God is Love?

January 20

I went back to the doctor for a checkup. Oddly, he says, the TB situation seems almost clear. It hardly makes sense, given the winter, the cold, etc. But he does not change his recommendation, nor the abbess her view.

January 25

Maybe anger is a tonic of sorts. I was really angry with the abbess about her refusal to reconsider. And I found myself thinking, "Well, if that's the way they are, I *can* live this elsewhere." Not that I want to, but I did sense a certain strength coming from the anger. Maybe my body really is getting better somehow.

February 2

Today is the anniversary of my entrance. I am not happy, but I do feel increasingly strong. It is true that I can live what I need to wherever I am. And if the God I know now is less benign than the God I thought I knew, well, that will be part of the process. There is getting to be some peace with living on the edge of the abyss. No departure date has been set yet, and I'm not asking. I'll just live day by day.

February 14

Apparently there was a council meeting, and the council asked the abbess at least to leave the question of departure open. I feel butterflies in my stomach—ten times magnified. Will she? What would that mean? This uncertainty is quite horrible to live, but I suppose I must live it. She isn't saying a thing.

March 1

I've lived the whole last three weeks on the edge of all this uncertainty. I hate it! However, maybe that's life—at least life here right now—living with uncertainty. I can hardly get through my food, but I know I have to try. Otherwise I'll never get better.

March 15

I had another medical exam. The doctor says I'm clear, and he waffles a bit now about my inability to live the life. The novice mistress is passing that on to the abbess.

March 17

There is silence from the abbess. I'm just swallowing my anger and living my life as I originally came to do—alone with God. I'll live what I need to . . . wherever, however.

March 19

The abbess called me this morning to say they—she and the council—had reconsidered. If I still wish to make Profession, I can go ahead and petition at the normal time. The community knows the problem, and this may make a difference to the votes, but I can go ahead.

I am simply numb. There is a kind of over-relaxation from relief, but I can't take it in yet. I just sit in my cell in a stupor.

March 25

This is the Feast of the Annunciation and my feast! It has a very new meaning for me now—as if a new life were given to me, a kind of challenge to start over, completely fresh. I still feel weak from all the emotional strain, but I am beginning to believe that more than one kind of spring can come.

Holy Thursday/ Good Friday

This year I know in a different way about darkness and death. Jesus' "Why have you forsaken me?" makes new sense. But that psalm ends in hope and triumph after all. Is that the way things eventually are? But there will be other deaths. And, I hope, new hope and new shapes of hope each time.

Easter

And so we rise . . . "If Christ be not risen from the dead we are of all people the most foolish." (1 Cor 15:19) I feel resurrected, too. But now I know why, after the resurrection, Christ still had his wounds. So do I.

May 15

After all the alarums and excursions, all the sweat and pain, it is getting on toward time to ask to be received for Profession. I do it with my heart in my mouth—not that I have any doubts any more: all the pain and struggle seem to have burned them away. But at moments I still need to think about things in the house—the pig-headedness in the Latin-vernacular fight, a certain closedness on the part of some, my own restlessness when others seem ignorant of the whole world-view outside. But the pain of the past months probably solidified my choice, and I expect to go ahead. Before I came, the abbess said to me, "The monastic life is the soul alone with God alone. Can you live that?" So however I may love people here and many things about the house, and however I may worry about others, ultimately that is what I'll be committing to when I petition for Profession. It's worth remembering.

June 13

The day when the Chapter votes on my Profession is approaching. After all the time I took wondering if I wanted to stay, I now ask myself: what if the community votes against me? The question has to be faced, though I'm told no one's name is presented at Chapter unless the person is expected to get through.

Still, I'm told that, beside the health issue, there are people in community and on the council who find me frightening or dangerous—too many new ideas, too progressive, whatever. Some people fear I might have leadership in that direction, and the community has just begun to heal its old wounds of division. Then there is the person—not alone, I fear—who thinks me an intellectual snob. (Too many bridge games at recreation!) The sad thing is, I really like her. My degree dogs me here: in a men's monastery it would just be normal. I hate that.

Do I really want to stay or is some of it relief over the new chance? By now, despite everything, I do think I want it very much. There are still the small annoyances, and the large ones. But there is also the wonder of a life wholly oriented to God—the depth and beauty of the liturgy; the deep peace in the house, in people, in the life-style; the real love I have found with so many. Yes, I want to stay. But I also know that people sense in me the ferment of a new age, a new theology and psychology. So will they vote against me? I asked the abbot president when he was here, and he said no. So whence my anxiety?

Maybe the more one wants or loves something the more one fears losing it. I came very close. I need to remember that what I need to live I can live—here or elsewhere, this way or another way. I need to be true to who I am and simply trust for the rest. Things will be as they are meant to be.

June 16

The Chapter accepted me. I can hardly believe it for joy. I had to write a petition saying why I wanted to make vows here and read it to the whole community. Talk about baring one's soul in public. But I did it honestly. The wait was hard but their answer, finally, was "yes." I feel as if I had been loved and accepted by each person in this house—for life. Maybe there were some black balls—who knows? But the community as a whole want me to stay. I vacillate between deep gratitude and peace and the awareness that now I have two months for a very serious spiritual preparation.

This latter boggles the mind. How can I possibly know what I am doing—this is all so much bigger than I am! I'm glad it's done at the Mass and is part of it, subsumed in something still bigger. In a way my preparation is hardly important before what objectively happens there. But I want to be as conscious, as present, as open to grace, as aware as I possibly can be.

Father Gregory can't do the ceremony: it has to be some VIP. Maybe the latter would delegate his authority to Father Mark, since he is an abbot. We'll see. These are not the important issues.

August 14

This is the eve of Profession and the end of retreat. I can't write about it and don't want to try. But I know this is what I want to do and have to do. The words of the ceremony are perfect: "Receive me, Lord, and I shall live. Do not disappoint me in my hope."

Profession Day

Deep peace! I don't want to talk or write about it. But this is what I needed to do. This is where I belong. Today is not an ending but a beginning. "Receive me, Lord, and I shall live . . ."

SECTION THREE: COMMENTARIES

This journal is a fantasy account of one woman's initiation process in one monastery. It borrows from reality, personal experience, the experience of others, interviews, reading. In the light of traditional anthropological insights, and then in the light of those of psychology, what is going on in such an experience? It can be looked at monastically, anthropologically, psychologically, personally. In this next section, I shall simply apply these different spotlights to the preceding material.

A Monastic Commentary

It is important at the beginning to look at this initiation process in the way in which a monastic would see it and in terms of what a monastic might say "should" be going on. To formulate this question in the language or categories of initiation, what is the space out of which this person is moving—monastically speaking—and what is the space into which she moves? Clearly the issue is not external stages—postulant, novice, professed—but rather inner stages. Several monastic writers touch on these questions.

In a book introducing the Cistercian life, its meaning and development in recent decades, Andre Louf writes:

> Above all there has been an attempt to restore the formative power of
> the monastic life itself for the monk. The ancient fathers had always
> been aware of this and had believed in it. But if the life itself is to form

the monk and to teach him the ways of God, then it must be adapted patiently and pliably to the work of grace in each one, and to the potential of each individual. Nowadays there is less tendency to impose a uniform life style worked out in advance on everyone. The aim is rather to stir up and nourish an interior liberty by which the Holy Spirit anticipates the work of man.[1]

The aim of the process is this movement into freedom, and Louf sees it as occurring through the experience of monastic life itself, seen as a liminal space after "leaving the world." Louf outlines its steps in terms of the experience of "leaving the world," coming to experience the life—its rhythm, its meaning—prayer, work, community, and the like. He especially stresses the growing experiences—growing in tandem—of personal weakness and of consciousness of the love of Christ. One can see in this outline the classical anthropological pattern of initiation: separation, liminality, entrance into community.

Another monk, a Benedictine abbot this time, writes in a set of letters to monks and nuns of his congregation:

> The way to live so that we are glad to be alive is what Benedict supposes we were all looking for when we entered the monastery, and what God offers us to meet that need is the experience of liberty in Christ . . . . I am concerned with the majority—whether among the novices or the professed—whose aim is the perpetual deepening of their inner liberty.[2]

Here, again, from a different source, we have a discussion of the importance of liberty. This is not, offhand, what most people think of when imagining monastic life. And the question of its relation to obedience will be dealt with below. If, however, one does not deeply—perhaps experientially—understand this element of inner liberty in monastic life, not only does one misunderstand the life but also it will be impossible to see any possible parallels with the experiences described in Part Two.

Huerre adds, in another place:

---

[1] Andre Louf, *The Cistercian Way*, N. Kinsella, trans. Cistercian Studies Series 76 (Kalamazoo: Cistercian, 1989) 43.

[2] Denis Huerre, *Letters to My Brothers and Sisters: Living by the Rule of St. Benedict*, S. Houdard, trans. (Collegeville: Liturgical Press, 1989) 22.

Actually, the principle of slow and gradual conversion applies even more to communities, since their maturity is marked by an absence of authoritarianism and by its members gaining the understanding and insight to avoid hangups—or at least gaining the ability to heal wounds once they are inflicted. The community that reaches this stage achieves a freedom which allows it to move forward into the future.[3]

This quotation is important as it speaks of liberty on the level of community—a description of a group of adults living the monastic way of life. Here maturity is seen in terms of understanding, insight, freedom from "hangups," notably around authority. The result of all this is not "no wounds" but rather ability to heal. Huerre gives an important key to the means to this end when he says "our aim is not to eliminate but to spiritualize what is human."[4] This is not about "spiritualizing" in the sense of denying the body. On the contrary, it implies the integration of all that is human, and that, once again, is an aim or purpose of this particular initiatory process. This is very important because the implication here is that it is a mistaken notion of monastic ascesis to try to destroy, repress, remove any aspect of one's human way of being. One could consider this to be the fruit of a mistaken form of initiatory process. What is removed from life and consciousness cannot be transformed. Where one meets religious people who are dried-up, wizened, half-alive—and one does—there has been a very different understanding of ascesis. And this refusal to eliminate anything human could probably be seen as the criterion of any healthy monastic spirituality.

In a set of lectures on spiritual guidance, Andre Louf speaks in more detail about the inner process of these initiatory years—notably from the point of view of those guiding the novice. He begins by giving the aim of the process:

Spiritual accompaniment will help us discover what we can call our interiority, that is to say our deep being, somewhere at the source of our being, which is not unconnected with the metaphysical place where the creating finger of God touches us and keeps us in existence at each moment. In each of us there is somewhere a place where God touches us.

[3] Ibid., 13.
[4] Ibid., 45.

The ancients call it the "place of God." At each moment we experience this touch of God which totally escapes our consciousness and our superficial sense awareness.[5]

He continues by saying that to find this place what is needed is not effort but a certain quiet and non-activity very difficult for most people. One could say that the whole discipline of the contemplative life is about learning this non-activity or quiet. God is always there, Louf comments, present to us "within." But, as Augustine says, we are not present there to God—nor to ourselves. And it is learning this presence that is the point of the whole process. In this description, the whole liminal process, sometimes described as "a desert experience," is precisely about learning this inner quiet, this non-activity. Many a spiritual tradition makes this same point. One can hardly avoid thinking of some parts of the Tao Te Ching.[6]

Free from desire, you realize the mystery.
Caught in desire, you see only the manifestations. (I)

Darkness with darkness.
The gateway to all understanding. (I)

Therefore the Master
Acts without doing anything
And teaches without saying anything.
Things arise and she lets them come;
Things disappear and she lets them go. (II)

Practice non-doing,
And everything will fall into place. (III)

The Tao is like a bellows:
It is empty yet infinitely capable . . .
Hold on to the center. (V)

We join spokes together in a wheel,
But it is the center hole
That makes the wagon move. (XI)

[5] Andre Louf, *Accompagnement Spirituel* (Ottowa: Editions de la Conference religieuse canadienne, 1986) 67. My trans. Henceforth referred to as *"AS."*

[6] *Tao Te Ching: a new English version with Foreword and Notes by Stephen Mitchell* (Harper Perennial, Harper Collins, 1991).

Empty your mind of all thoughts.
Let your heart be at peace.
Watch the turmoil of beings,
But contemplate their return. (XVI)

Paradoxically, this inner silence or emptiness is precisely about finding
a fullness that is there but unrecognized if one is superficial. Louf speaks
of the place of God. Buddhists speak of the Buddha-nature. Hindus say
"That art Thou." This is what the monastic quest in all traditions is about.

And yet, even more paradoxically, one finds this inner quiet only by
owning up to what is least quiet within one. Louf speaks at once of the
old monastic tradition of "manifestation of thoughts"—a process not dissimilar ultimately from psychoanalysis in its demand for complete openness—and a process many a novice in Orthodox monasteries enters into
daily. What Louf stresses about this process is the need for the novice to
experience being received as she is with love, without any judgment, excuses, or reassurances. A different attitude might lead the novice to push
aside some of his or her desires or negative attitudes, he comments, and
what is pushed out of consciousness cannot be transformed.

Two inner phenomena need to be analyzed, he comments. One is the
inner policemen whom Freudians call the superego. The other is the mirror—the God I create as a mirror of myself. The process of spiritual
growth will involve the movement toward freedom from the first as opposed to a more personal judgment or morality and the purification of
the God-image from the second.

Louf's clear familiarity with psychological language may indicate already here some links with the material to come in Part Two.[7]

Several monastics in charge of novices have commented that the primary things they look for before proposing someone for profession are
(1) the ability to do one's own inner work (which does not imply that
there is no consultation) and (2) the fact that the person has interiorized
what the whole monastic "thing" is about. The "I could live this even
elsewhere" of the journal and the monk's ability to remain "monk" even
when dressed in "civvies" and in a totally non-monastic environment are
part of this. The "monk thing" is not a persona: it is a way of being. The

---

[7] *AS,* passim.

process of initiation—mostly by the life—as described in the journal is about getting to this point.

From the viewpoint of various religious traditions, Raymond Pannikar writes of the "monk archetype":

> By monk, *monachos,* I understand that person who aspires to reach the ultimate goal of life with all his being by renouncing all that is not neces- sary to it, i.e. by concentrating on this one single and unique goal. . . . The monk is at least in the state of *mumuksutra,* or desire to be liber- ated. . . . The thesis I am defending is that the monk is the expression of an archetype which is a *constitutive dimension of human life* . . . . The monk ultimately becomes monk not by a process of thinking (about death, the caducity of all things, *nitya* . . .), or merely of desiring (God, human perfection, heaven, *nirvana* . . .), but as the result of an urge, the fruit of an experience that eventually leads him to change, and, in the final analysis, break something in his life *(conversio, metanoia, ihamu- trarthaphala bhoga-viragah* . . .) for the sake of that "thing" which en- compasses or transcends everything (the pearl, brahman, peace, *shama, moksa,* liberation, God, *satori,* enlightenment . . . .[8]

This description tells us what the process is about. Once again here we see the goal of this particular initiatory process and we see the cost in terms of a "break" with the old and a liminal experience—ongoing con- version. Pannikar uses the rest of his book to explain that where in previ- ous ages this process took place largely by exclusion, contemporary "monks" (in monasteries or not) see it more in terms of inclusion, inte- gration. Dealing with this idea in detail would take us too far afield, but it relates to Huerre's remark about the spiritualization of the human.

Pannikar's comments speak to us of the universality of the monk- archetype. What is said here about monasticism and described in a mo- nastic journal is in fact the human experience of seeking and longing for the essential—a longing that leads some people into analysis, some into monasteries, and others into other forms of search. It is the longing at the center of the human psyche, which Jung would call the desire for individ- uation and Augustine described as the search for God.

---

[8] Raimundo Pannikar, *Blessed Simplicity: the Monk as Universal Archetype* (New York: Seabury, 1982) 10–11.

The comments above about the importance of interiorization are significant here as well. If the monastic archetype is present in everyone, the monastic devotes the whole of his or her life to its realization. The strangeness or "otherness" of the life and ascesis experienced at the time of entering needs gradually to develop into a space where the monastic understands the significance of and the reason for the different "practices" of the monastic life. This makes possible the development of what some call the *sens monastique*—a kind of monastic instinct that knows what fits and what does not with the life that has been chosen. For the mature monastic the responsibility of his or her choices belongs to him or her. It is ineluctable. So either initiation develops in the initiand this monastic heart and attitude or the whole process does not "take"—which obviously can occur. In summary, then, where do the five "moments" of the liminal phase occur according to classical monastic theology?

(1) The whole time of formation is an ordeal. The life is a radical change from the past and is normally experienced as quite austere—fasting, silence, enclosure, shorter sleep, obedience, often cold, the stress of community living without the normal outlets and escapes. These are the "rough paths" of which the novice master or mistress warns the candidate. There can be other ordeals, as described in the journal, but, in fact, the life itself—especially at first—is the ordeal.

(2) Obedience to the elders is largely about obedience to the novice master/mistress and abbot/abbess, who, in turn (3) pass on the tradition or see that it is passed on in classes and in (4) spiritual guidance. (5) The connection with a sacred space occurs in prayer, sacred reading, liturgy at first, but then it becomes a matter of all of life as in Benedict's comment that every utensil in the monastery should be used like a vessel on the altar.

But before moving on to an anthropological look at monastic initiation, one more question needs to be answered. In psychological terms, is the whole monastic venture a "deviation," a collective neurosis, a process opposed to that of individuation? And entirely aside from celibacy, what about obedience? And so we need a short digression.

Digression: Monastic Obedience, Celibacy, Ascesis

If there is one aspect of the monastic life that is perfectly incomprehensible from outside and especially from the psychological point of view, it is obedience, for is obedience not the antithesis of individuation? (And it is worth commenting that the Greek adage "the worst is the corruption of the best" applies perfectly here—in terms of the caricatures one sees.) How can one live the inner liberty discussed above in a framework stressing obedience as the monastic life does?

From a rational point of view this question is absolutely correct. But why, then, so much talk about liberty in the preceding pages? One of the fundamental tenets of monastic, ascetical theology is that there are, so to speak, two wills in humans. There is the deep God-seeking will and the superficial will manifested in self-will, pride, attachments, what the medievals called "cupidity" or "concupiscence." They even had a saying, *Concupiscentia est infinita.*

Translated, that means that there is no limit to greed, avarice, selfishness, and selfish desires. When Benedict's first degree of humility states, "Truly, we are forbidden to do our own will" moderns shake their heads in horror. But that "will"—often called *voluntas propria*—is not one's deep will but the superficial self-will that militates against one's own deepest being as well. The whole discipline of obedience to an "abba" or "amma" in the desert—or in an Orthodox monastery—was about the giving up of this self-will and selfish desires. One efficient and drastic way to do this was by the absolute obedience required. Taken correctly, this whole process can in itself be an initiation. Into the void—or liminal space—created by this renunciation of self-will comes the directive of a wiser and freer judgment that in time frees the novice from some old habits. The same can be said of the Eastern traditions concerning the importance of a *guru* or *roshi*—though these views, like those of Western monasticism, can be taken wrong or go awry.

This is one aspect of monastic obedience. There are two others. The first will be understandable to anyone who has married or lived at length closely committed to others. When people live together there is a common good. My good must be considered but, if I value the whole, so must the whole. A husband may not like doing the family laundry, but this may be his fair share of the load. This is simply human.

But the final level, the most "mystical," is also the most difficult. The Christian paradigm is the Christ. Christ's supreme "moment of glory" was the Cross/Resurrection experience that is called the "Paschal Mystery"—a mystery of life through death. In deeper human experience there is awareness of this archetypal reality or law.

Psychologically healthy people do not normally *seek* suffering or cruci-fixion. That would be dolorism or masochism. But one can be sure that in the course of any committed human experience such moments will come. Think of the man whose wife is in an accident, the mother whose child "goes wrong," the lover who finally realizes the relationship cannot continue though he or she would deeply wish it to. These are deaths and some monastic deaths come through obedience. Some, not all. It is a life understood in terms of the Paschal Mystery.

It is necessary, also, to say in this context that it is all too possible for situations surrounded by the "mystique" of obedience to become abu-sive. Everything depends on the outlook, theology, and personality of the person exercising authority. I have lived at length in monastic communi-ties where I never saw any abusive use of power. I have lived in others where abuse was truly daily bread. This is an issue that will increasingly need to be addressed as our consciousness of the meaning and extent of abuse increases.

A word only about the mystique of celibacy as well. Suffice it to say here that celibacy is not about suppression of sexual energy but its redi-rection. The plethora of early and medieval commentaries on the Song of Songs shows well enough this understanding of celibacy as a choice of a specific love or eros.

The risk, of course, is the denial or underrating of the body, sexuality, passion, and this whole aspect of the human. But celibacy need not be lived thus. Rabbi Akiba is supposed to have said that if the whole of Scrip-ture except the Song of Songs were lost, the Song would be enough.

THE AIM OF IT ALL: JOHN CASSIAN[9]

A final word, before ending this monastic discussion of the Journal, to look at what the earliest Christian monks in the desert saw as the aim of monastic initiation. John Cassian and his friend Germanus went around the desert consulting the "Ancients" or "Abbas" about their way of life. In true Socratic fashion, Abba Moses asks them: what is the end or purpose of monastic life? When they answer, somewhat vaguely, "the Kingdom of God," he replies:

[9] See John Cassian, *Conferences,* Colm Luibheid, trans. Classics of Western Spiritu-ality (New York/Mahwah: Paulist, 1985).

The aim of our profession is the kingdom of God, or the kingdom of heaven. But our point of reference, our objective, is a clean heart, without which it is impossible for anyone to reach our target. . . . without this the goal cannot be reached. . . . Therefore, we must follow completely anything that can bring us to this objective, to this purity of heart, and anything which pulls us away from it must be avoided. . . . What is this [love] and its like if not the continuous offering to God of a heart that is perfect and truly pure, a heart kept free of all disturbance? . . . We do [all] to hold our hearts free of the harm of every dangerous passion and in order to rise step by step to the high point of love.[10]

It is interesting that he relates purity of heart, and so, the point of the whole way of life, with peace and with love. A millennium later Bernard of Clairvaux will speak of the need of ordering one's love (read: one's affectivity as well as one's will and choices) in order to move from the "bent" position of fallen humanity to the straightness of the child of God made in God's image.[11] It is, then, about recovering one's full (divinized) humanity as opposed to living basically tied up in the knots of one's complexes, passions, and sins. As we shall see below, Jung speaks of the birth of the divine child in the psyche as Campbell later says that the hero, after going through his ordeals, moves to a level of "superconsciousness," which could also be called deeper consciousness. A single intuition seems to be at work in much of this thought. It concerns the purpose of life as well as the purpose of initiation, and it is about becoming who or what one most deeply is, being in touch with one's deepest desires, being who or what one is called to be.   *individuation*

Jung Quote

Anthropological Commentary

Some basic anthropological concepts concerning initiation were discussed in the introduction to this book and section. Therefore they will not be repeated here. A brief discussion of the preceding journal in terms

[10] Ibid., 39.

[11] See Etienne Gilson, *The Mystical Theology of St. Bernard*, A.H.C. Downes, trans. Cistercian Studies Series 120 (Kalamazoo: Cistercian, 1990). Henceforth referred to as "Gilson."

of the three major headings of rupture, liminality, and integration into the community and its myths will suffice.

As far as the first is concerned, one could certainly say that the moment of walking through the cloister door as described on February 1 is the moment of rupture as well as of entrance into liminality. The person entering has left the whole world that she knew, her whole previous experience, and, by the very fact of the enclosure, she is separated from everyone and everything in that life quite drastically. The disorientation of the first weeks and months is the deepening of this experience and of the liminality. The candidate is no longer part of the world she has left, and yet she is not yet part of that into which she has come. (A monk once told me: "It takes ten years to make a monk." That is a rather long liminality!) She finds all the things she came to seek apparently absent from her. The surprisingly exasperating details of community living become increasingly intense. She is forced to reconsider this option and wonder if it is truly right for her.

Within this "desert" or liminal space, the journal records experiences of "input" meant to be potentially transforming and which we have listed as essentials to the experience of liminality:

1) There are the liturgical experiences referred to around Christmas, Easter, even the negative experience of Lent;

2) There are the conversations with abbess, novice mistress, abbot (Mark), spiritual guide (Gregory);

3) There is above all the long, frequently "desert," experience of simply living the life with its ups and downs, its annoyances and joys; (one monk commented to me that his own formation consisted almost entirely of becoming part of this rhythm: he rarely spoke with his novice master;)

4) There is the real ordeal of dealing with daily petty annoyances that can really grind a person down (neighbor's raucous singing; other people's reactions): the monastic setting makes some such experiences much harder to escape than other settings—leading up to a final major ordeal;

5) There are the moments of very serious decision—petitioning for the habit or vows and then the moment of commitment itself—which, in the latter case, terminates the formal time of initiation;

6) And, of course, there are classes, conferences, reading, and much else.

One does find, through this process, a growth in her own development and inner liberty, a growth in spiritual maturity, and independence from external circumstances—a process that is as much about psychology as anthropology. For one thing she moves from indecision into a place where she can choose this commitment with freedom. For another, paradoxically, she also decides that she must be her own person—even should this endanger her acceptance—and that she has sufficiently interiorized the whole experience so that she could, if need be, live it elsewhere. She moves out of an obsessive exasperation with local irritations to a point where they lose a lot of their significance so that the forest becomes more important than the trees. She comes to a point of reformulating her faith-understanding in a newer and deeper way. She moves, then, to a more centered position that, phenomenologically, is described as "peace." By the time she comes to a final commitment, she has truly become part of this new community in an interiorized way hardly possible except by the painful living through of this whole process and ordeal.

Psychological Commentary

FUNDAMENTAL MONASTIC ARCHETYPES

Having seen the monastic experience of initiation from a monastic point of view what could be said if one reconsiders the material using the tools or spotlight of analytical psychology?

One of the best ways, within this tradition, of looking at an initiatory experience in general and a monastic one in particular is to consider which are the archetypes involved in the experience.

Jung's thought about archetypes evolved through three basic stages. Early on, he spoke of "universal images that have existed since the remotest times,"[12] "representations collectives," appearing in myths and fairy tales. Later, he begins to speak more of their psychosomatic reality and the distinction between the archetype itself and its images. Archetypes are at the core of our complexes and "link body and psyche, instinct and image."[13] In his later years, Jung stressed the manifold expressions of

[12] CW IXi, 5.

[13] Andrew Samuels, Bani Shorter, and Fred Plaut, *A Critical Dictionary of Jungian Analysis* (London: Routledge, 1986) 26. Henceforth referred to as "Samuels," 26.

an archetype which make it, in fact, indefinable.[14] In a monastic setting, the archetypes would be expressed in the only partially conscious images and symbols that give meaning and impetus to the whole monastic process. I suggest that the basic motifs or archetypal images would be (A) the return to paradise, (B) the Night Sea Journey—largely in its Christian formulation as the Paschal Mystery, (C) the sacred marriage, (D) the divine child within, growing into the son/daughter of God, (E) the wise old man or woman, (F) and, fundamental to it all, the *shadow*, as experienced in the monastic notion of humility. We will first look briefly at these archetypes and then in more depth see them working.

Is there some relationship between these archetypes and what were called above five basic elements of the liminal stage of initiation? It would be nice if there were an easy fit, but things are not that easy. The *paradisus claustralis* of which Merton speaks following Bernard[15] is the end of a long process of dealing with one's *shadow*, becoming tolerant of one's own failings and thus compassionate with those of others. In this connection one could say that coming to humility—the fruit of dealing with the *shadow*—was the essential monastic ordeal (notably with Benedict's understanding of all the trials it involves) and that the finding of monastic *peace*, or a beginning of *paradise*, was about finding the sacred source as one moves on in the process.

Humility, according to the Rule of Benedict, shows itself in obedience to the elders and a readiness to receive the traditions of the community and be open with one's spiritual guide.[16] The reader will recognize the elements of initiation pointed out above. These will be recognized as aspects of the liminal stage. The experience of humility will lead one through a veritable *Night Sea Journey* or union with the death of Christ leading to a resurrection. It will lead to the growth of the *divine child* within, to wisdom, or, to change the metaphor, to *the sacred marriage* (a term used more in later monastic literature). Thus we see the profound interweaving of the archetypal themes in monasticism with the aspects of the liminal

[14] CW IXi, 80.

[15] *Siloe*, ch. 14.

[16] *RB 1980: The Rule of St. Benedict in Latin and English with Notes*, T. Fry et al., eds. (Collegeville: Liturgical Press, 1981). Henceforth referred to as *RB 1980*. References are to 7:55.

stage. In this way one can see the interplay of the archetypes involved in monastic living as well as the initiatory movement through ordeal and liminality toward a new space or way of being.

The diagram in Figure One shows this progression in a clockwise form, although this presents the disadvantage of having the transformative results all be "in the sky," whereas they are far more in the depths. The advantage to the circular movement is that it allows one to think in terms of cycles: wisdom is not won once for all, nor is paradise. One repeats the Night Sea Journey.

Figure One also shows that the impetus which sets the whole process in motion is, in monastic terms, humility, and in Jungian terms, confronting the archetype of the shadow. In Benedictine monasticism the development of humility is the key to the whole process of living the life. In Jung's thought, work with the shadow is the *sine qua non* for any psychological development that may follow. One could say that this is the most profound point of convergence for these two kinds of thought.

Let us look at some of these monastic archetypes in greater depth. This discussion, too, must be cyclical—for that is how these experiences progress.

Figure One

One could see this as a mandala with the Self at the center, regulating.

I believe that one could make a good case for a *return to paradise* as a fundamental monastic archetype—especially in the West. Benedict's Prologue speaks in the earliest paragraphs of the "return by obedience to God from whom we have strayed by the vice of disobedience" (read: disordered self-will or attachment.) The fault most criticized in the Rule is "murmuring," which, it will be remembered, is what kept the Israelites in the desert rather than leading them to the Promised Land. Jerusalem, the "City of Peace" image is a leading one in Scripture as the promise finally fulfilled, then lost, destroyed, longed for, restored, and finally seen increasingly symbolically (e.g., "the heavenly Jerusalem . . . the assembly of the first-born who are enrolled in heaven" [Heb 12:22-23]).

In religious imagery, the Exodus theme moves forward into what Christians see it as prefiguring—the Paschal Mystery (through death into glory) and indeed the Exodus journey begins with the sacrifice of the Paschal Lamb whose blood is protection for beginning the journey from slavery to freedom.

Underlying these images are those of Eden—the earthly paradise, lost in the past but symbol of a promised future. The medieval Cistercian writers were also to stress this theme of return to Paradise, of fallen/"bent" humans again becoming "straight" without ever forgetting their fallenness.[17] Even the famous Benedictine "Peace" motto is about this return to paradise.

What is the psychological significance of this rich imagery? A well-known psychologist of religion, Antoine Vergote,[18] accuses monasticism, mysticism—and Jung!—of furthering some sort of "oceanic mysticism," a return to the mother and the womb, rather than a response to the father's call to personal responsibility and ethical behavior as in Freud. Jung does indeed speak of the necessity of healing regression, and it is even clear that creative expression finds its source in these "waters" (rather than in ethics!). But it is important to distinguish the lost paradise of the womb, of Eden, from the paradise regained which we are discussing here and which never forgets the existence of darkness and sin—and the other aspects of reality—coexisting with this new joy.

[17] Gilson, 44–59.
[18] See Antoine Vergote, *The Religious Man: a Psychological Study of Religious Attitudes,* M-B Said, trans. (Dublin: Gill and Macmillan, 1969).

What underlies the specifically Christian imagery of the Paschal Mystery is the older nature symbolism of the Night Sea Journey—the sun reborn each morning and dying each night. The yearly cycle of seasons with the death-imagery of winter and the spring rebirth has been recaptured in one early myth after another. What is specific to its Christian form is what the Epistle to the Hebrew stresses as *"once"*—Christ died once, sins are repaired once, the resurrection is once for all. The historical replaces the cyclical.

But only partially. Through the Liturgy of the Hours (the Office), the monastic sings or chants each morning of the birth of the day, the end of night (often seen as the domain of darkness or sin), the beginning of color and movement, the coming of the sun, seen as a Christ-symbol. The unfolding of the work of creation as seen in Genesis is celebrated with its culmination in the human. In the evening the end of day is sung, the end of work, the coming of night, calm, rest, and there is prayer against the temptations of the dark (depression, fear, and also what is seen as sexual temptation).

The yearly cycle also uses these levels of imagery—the natural, the universally human, underlying the more specifically Christian. The winter cold and darkness is seen as a time of waiting for the fulfillment of a long-deferred promise. Right after the winter solstice (the Roman *sol invictus,* unconquered sun) comes the night celebration of the birth of Christ-light, breaking open the darkness with angel-songs of joy and peace. In Jungian language one might speak, sociologically, of a first awareness of the Self after centuries of darkness or, individually, after the long dark of immersion in the collective.

The next great night—the Paschal celebration—is again inserted in the cold time of winter's end. Religiously it is prepared for by a long fast, a long ascesis, and—with Holy Thursday / Good Friday—a celebration of evening as conviviality, friendship, love turning into an experience of betrayal, trial, torture, abandonment, death. Stark liturgical symbols are used these last days before the night when fire is blessed and Exultation (the famous *Exultet* with its "O happy fault!") chanted. The whole history of the human race is covered in Scripture vignettes leading to a final explosion of joy with bells, music, and alleluias, silenced for forty days before. This vigil's review of the whole of human history is like a reliving of what the race is about, what life is about—all of which culminates in the dramatic re-presentation of the death-rebirth Paschal Mystery. The reliving of this whole history and experience, year after year, is in itself an initiatory experience.

This Lent-Easter cycle is also specifically an annual entrance into death by stages—ascesis, fasting, awareness of human suffering not one's own, then (hopefully!) awareness of all the varying facets of human suffering and pain across the globe and through the centuries. One could call this also an initiatory separation and movement into liminality. What is meant to be experienced at Easter is the transformation of all this, not only in the Resurrection but also in new birth as seen in the water/baptism symbolism of the whole week. What emerges is meant to be not only a renewed person but also a renewed community if one thinks in initiatory terms.

This liturgical "digression" is important because it is the warp and woof of a monastic life (even of a Christian life). This daily, weekly, yearly rhythm is meant to serve as what Jung calls a transforming symbol—a complex of such symbols, forming a whole and changing the psyche of participants, as living myths do, in a way that provides meaning and, ultimately, transformation.

All of this is about a life, a structure. On the more individual level one could say that two other archetypes operate—in different degrees for different people. One is the biblical symbolism of marriage and union as expressed in the Song of Songs. This image is used over and over again in monastic commentaries from Origen through the Cistercians and John of the Cross.

What is the connection between this imagery and Jung's sacred marriage? Jung defines this latter as the union between conscious and unconscious,[19] but he also sees it within the whole tradition of mystical marriage as described, notably, in alchemy.

From a Christian theological point of view is it the union of conscious and unconscious that is the issue? Considering that the "objective unconscious" includes everything that human consciousness does not or cannot take in, one might consider the two concepts coextensive. On the other hand, if theologians from the Pseudo-Areopagite to Meister Eckhart say that one cannot even postulate being of a God beyond all being, can one

---

[19] CW XIV, ch. 6.

postulate "the unconscious"? One must really wonder. The Christian "sacred marriage" is about a relationship with a God beyond all conceptualization. In psychological language speaking of awareness of the Self as a unifying and ordering principle on the deepest level might be more to the point of what is being said.

Another basic but related archetype profoundly related to transformation is that of the divine child—new birth—becoming a child of God. This symbolism is preferred by people who find the kind of nuptial imagery just discussed less attractive. It is easy to see how this personal experience is fed by the material mentioned above—the notions of death leading to rebirth and, in fact, the new birth brought by each day.

It is also easy to see how the symbolism we are discussing connects with that of the wise old man or woman of which Jung often speaks. At the end of chapter 7 of the Rule—a chapter that could be considered a central expression of Benedict's spirituality—is the statement:

> Now, therefore, after ascending all these steps of humility, the monk will quickly arrive at that perfect love of God which casts out fear (1 Jn 4:18). Through this love, all that he once performed with dread, he will now begin to observe without effort, as though naturally, from habit, no longer out of fear of hell, but out of love for Christ, good habit and delight in virtue. All this the Lord will by the Holy Spirit graciously manifest in his workman now cleansed of vices and sins.[20]

One could say that this is Benedict's description of his "wise old man"—someone free from fear, free in love and in love of virtue, someone in whom all this has been done, as opposed to being something he has done in himself. This whole picture has to do with the archetype of wisdom which recurs in various images throughout the Rule—notably in the portrayal of the abbot, the spiritual elders, and the notion that the monk or nun is personally on a movement toward a transformation such as the one described above and is seen in terms of wisdom.

The fact that this archetype of wisdom springs out of the very central chapter on humility also shows the primary importance of the shadow archetype that could, as was said, be considered the bedrock of the whole monastic process. In basing his whole ascesis on humility, Benedict guar-

---

[20] *RB 1980*, ch. 7, conclusion.

antees that shadow material—and shadow material acknowledged—must be at its heart. A great many monastic customs like the chapter of faults, the already mentioned manifestation of thoughts, the reverence shown to others by physical signs like bows and many others have their roots in the centrality of this issue.

This factor is deepened by the daily recitation of the psalter especially when this is done in one's own language. It is difficult to have too etherial a notion of the spiritual path when one is daily singing or reciting poetry which is full, not only of sublime images of nature, beauty, trust, love but also of the most gut-wrenching hate, vengefulness, and despair. It is interesting that while the Church's official Liturgy of the Hours has removed the more vindicative and imprecatory language from the psalter, most monastic communities have not gone along with this "purification."

Having looked at the significance of these various symbols and archetypes, it is worth taking a moment to see this whole movement as expressed in the journal. The writer's liminal experience begins with her entrance that is almost immediately followed by a first, relatively light, "Night" experience when the whole life seems to lose its significance and purpose. Though she is living a certain openness to the tradition and a daily obedience to what is asked of her, it seems as if an important decision in these early days is the willingness to be open about what she is feeling and experiencing, even at the risk of being told she is in the wrong place. This is a turning point in her process because it is about avowing who one really is. In Benedict's chapter on humility, coming to this readiness is an essential step in one's growth. And, of course, in the realm of psychology, such openness is what analysis is all about. In both cases what is involved is coming to terms with the reality of one's being.

At key moments in the journal she again expresses her doubts and questions to people, but the real, personal crisis and Night comes in the health problem of the last six months. Here it looks as if everything she has come to during these initiatory years is now at risk of being lost. This experience forces her into an interiorization and personalization of the entire process that is, in fact, contrary to how it feels, a deepening.

One could not say that she reaches wisdom, transformation, spiritual marriage but there are first glimmers of all of these. Hopefully, she has the rest of her life to grow along these lines, which will, again, occur through other Nights and cycles of development.

As was said, the liturgy and liturgical year can supply a means of reliving not only the Judaeo-Christian tradition but even the whole religiously-understood history of the human race. This is done quite explicitly in the Holy Saturday night vigil. The references to liturgical events in the journal are clear: Lent (April 1), Easter (after April 1), Jerusalem symbolism (June 29), Christmas, Lent again (March 20). The comments on a conference (May 30) show the significance of "liturgical living" in her understanding of her way of life. Again, the decisive importance of the personal event of the Clothing (August 14) is important as well. A radical inner experience connects, here, with an external ceremony that gave it its meaning and importance. I can say, from personal experience and that of others, that this is very far from being always the case. One can go through such a ceremony like an automaton—or with many questions. In her case, which archetypes are touched? I believe that it was not only Pannikar's monastic archetype—though certainly that—but deeper still, the archetype of the Self, in connection with whom/what in her deep being she feels drawn to come. This is a decisive moment in the journal.

THE WORKING OF THESE ARCHETYPES

We have seen the theory of the archetypes underlying monastic life, theology, initiation. How do these archetypes function in the daily experience of the monastic life? A few short examples will suffice.

The Night Sea Journey or Paschal Mystery is a constant. It occurs in the act of entering a monastery (which Merton compared to the belly of Jonah's whale), i.e., leaving everything, and entering into a life of obedience. This can be an activity, also, which opens one to the "feminine," surrendering, more passive and receptive activity of the psyche.

But the risk would lie in the tendency to remain in this space—passively obedient, childishly trustful, projecting all light onto external authority—of which more in the following sub-section. But it is also a phase necessary to transformation.

Nor is the Night Sea Journey a phase passed through once and for all. Spiritual desolation, misunderstanding and criticism, difficult obedience, losses, and many other factors figure here. Yearly, for example, everyone in a monastery gives up his or her "job"—to see whether, in a day or two, that job or another will be given back. This is true for everyone in the house and can be a real death experience for someone very "attached" (for good or ill) to a certain work—be it training novices, working with re-treatants, gardening, farming, or whatever. This yearly "death" is meant to serve as a reminder that the monk or nun is more important than any work he or she does, that inner detachment matters more than produc-tion, but it can be a painful experience, among many others.

We have connected this imagery with that of a kind of immersion in the cycles of nature—daily, weekly, yearly. How does this last work itself out?

Jung speaks of the early ages of the human race as being a time of "participation mystique"—an unconscious oneness with nature. There is, of course, a kind of nature mysticism along these lines (sometimes attrib-uted—very unfairly!—to Francis of Assisi) that can be found in various forms all around us. The monastic liturgy, and the Liturgy of the Hours, hardly further this state, nor does one find it frequently in monastic circles. What one does find, interestingly, is a kind of aesthetics that re-spects natural products—wood, stone, even concrete in its way. One monk commented to me that a monastery ought to fit into its natural environ-ment so well as to be hardly noticeable.

On a deeper level, there is a sense of harmony with nature that is not un-conscious but deeply felt. I think of the Monastery of Christ in the Desert where the first office (Vigils) is so timed that it begins in darkness and ends just as the first rays of the sun emerge from behind the canyon. I think of the Easter celebration at Glastonbury, timed the same way—these among dozens more. When this works well, it can lead to the kind of love of natu-ral beauty found throughout the writings of a Thomas Merton, for example.

All this relates to the notions of paradise and return to paradise on which Mario Jacoby has commented at length.[21] Jacoby sees the desire for paradise in the classical sense of the desire to return to the mother. Where the primal relationship was insufficient, the longing for paradise replaces the ability to live in reality, for "life's reality is . . . perceived as the devouring or castrating environment mother."[22] Paradise is the state of innocence—that is to say, not a state without guilt but a state without conscious guilt. Jacoby gives the ex-ample of a child being innocent, not because it never hurts its mother, but because it does this without knowing what it does. With the emergence of

---

[21] Mario Jacoby, *Longing for Paradise: Psychological Perspectives on an Archetype*, (Boston: Sigo Press, 1985).

[22] Ibid., 108.

conscious guilt comes the emergence of conscience, the "knowledge of good and evil" of the Fall. Jacoby follows Winnicott concerning the development of conscience at around six months, in its inchoate stage.

> . . . a mother who is capable of harmonizing her feelings and actions with her child's internal realities and needs and does not impose external training measures prematurely, encourages the child's essential ability to be able at a later time in its life to listen to its own inner voice, the 'voice of conscience.' That conscience is felt as a sense of guilt whenever there is a deviation from that primal order . . . . it sounds the alarm whenever the intentions of ego-consciousness deviate too far from the primal order of human existence (the *self*, in the Jungian sense of the word).[23]

In this psychological sense, then, the desire to return to paradise is a desire for the "good-enough mothering" one never had. This point will be returned to in the next sub-section where "the dark side" is discussed. Here, however, it seems important to see what is applicable to monasticism and what is not.

One can hardly deny that a monastic vocation based on a longing for paradisiac peace could indeed be an effort to find what was denied in childhood. The longing for peace lies deep in the human psyche—and the more, where childhood was deprived. Unfortunately (or fortunately), monasteries do not supply this kind of peace. There is indeed a serenity that can come from a life of balance and rhythm. But there are also the boundless difficulties coming from the austerity of the life, the pinpricks—or worse—from others, the difficulties with oneself, and one could go on.

It rapidly becomes clear that any peace that is attained will have to be not "despite" but somehow "including" all this. The early desert theology spoke of "apatheia"—a term taken from the Stoics but meant rather differently. To translate it as "passionlessness" is to miss the point. *Pathein* is about suffering, being passive. "*A-*" is a negative; so it would be truer to say this is a way of being where one is less susceptible to being invaded by suffering, passion, or events, which is not at all to say one is insensitive to them.

Is this a denial of feeling, a repression? No, it is rather an acceptance, a consciousness, but in the peace of self-acceptance. The section of the Rule immediately preceding the one quoted to describe the wise person reads:

---

[23] Ibid., 132. Jacoby is here following D. W. Winnicott.

Judging himself always guilty on account of his sins, he should consider
that he is already at the fearful judgment and constantly say in his heart
what the publican in the Gospel said with downcast eyes: Lord, I am a
sinner, not worthy to look up to heaven (Luke 18:13).[24]

Lugubrious, many would say, but it is followed immediately with the notion of the fearlessness of perfect love—a beautiful example of the interaction of opposites.

So this is not the peace or the paradise of innocence, of an unspotted
conscience. It is not attained by a return in dream or fantasy or projection
to the Mother. Rather, it is about moving on through recognized guilt to
forgiveness and self-forgiveness to love and freedom.

The last, more individual, archetypes discussed have more to do with
the individual—nuptial imagery, adoption imagery, wisdom imagery.
John Dourley discusses the first in detail in terms of the writings of
Mechthilde of Magdeburg. A few quotations he takes from her writings
can serve as sufficient commentary here.

> I must to God—
> My Father through nature,
> My Brother through humanity,
> My Bridegroom through love, His am I forever.

> Then the beloved goes into the lover,
> into the secret hiding place of the sinless Godhead . . . .
> and there, the soul being fashioned in the very nature of God, no
>   hindrance can come between it and God.

> Now comes a blessed stillness
> Welcome to both, He gives Himself to her
> And she to Him
> What shall befall her, the soul knows:
> Therefore am I comforted.[25]

All this is right in the tradition of the nuptial literature already mentioned
above from Origen on about the *Song*. For some this can be symbolism

[24] *RB 1980*, ch. 7, degree 12 of humility.

[25] John P. Dourley, *Love, Celibacy and the Inner Marriage* (Toronto: Inner City Books, 1987) 33.

that explains their "journey." Others prefer the wisdom imagery or what the Eastern Church speaks of as "deification." In any case, such symbolism functions as a kind of guiding or explanatory imagery to explain a process difficult to understand but summarized in the one basic criterion Benedict gives for a monastic vocation: does the person truly seek God?

THE DARK SIDE

In a 1983 novel about psychoanalysis Rossner describes the husband from whom her heroine separates:

> He was also a man whose excellent brain had become ossified from inadequate exposure to the air outside the New York Psychoanalytic Institute . . . . a man for whom the Freudian prism had been a comfortable prison, a refuge from the very truths it revealed as well as from those it didn't encompass; a man who, by remaining exactly the same for eighteen years, had deteriorated steadily in her eyes.[26]

This description, unfortunately, fits all too well some whose brains can become ossified by too many years in what Erving Goffman describes in *Asylums* as a "total institution"—"a place of residence and work where a large number of like-situated individuals, cut off from the wider society for an appreciable period of time, together lead an enclosed, formally administered round of life."[27] Obviously, enclosed communities, notably of women where the enclosure is stricter, are prime candidates for this problem—though a French priest in charge of religious life in his diocese once commented: "My quarrel with the monasteries is that they take a perfectly normal young man and turn him into a museum piece."

On a deeper level, a part of what can be responsible for this phenomenon is a tendency to project the Self onto the monastery (if not the superior). It then becomes the worst of crimes to criticize, even to question, anything going on there. And there is no need at all to seek for knowledge, understanding or self-knowledge, self-understanding—anywhere else. Newspapers, magazines, psychology, philosophy, outside relationships can all become enemies. "We don't need any of this: we have God; God is enough."

[26] Judith Rossner, *August* (New York: Warner Books, 1983) 43.

[27] Erving Goffman, *Asylums: essays on the Social Situation of Mental Patients and Other Inmates,* Anchor Books (Garden City, N.Y.: Doubleday, 1961) xiii.

God is indeed enough. The question is, however, does a lack of awareness of what is going on in the world, including its suffering and its crises, further the search for God? Two things need to be said here. One is that individual vocations differ tremendously—even in a single monastery. One person can be deeply compassionate and open and never need a newspaper. Another can turn each page of a paper into prayer. But, on the other hand, one can fall into either of two extremes—losing oneself in a search for information that leaves no inner space for God, or, on the other hand, lapsing into a lazy and comfortable ignorance that is hardly a space for God.

A certain amount of "ideologizing" about monastic life can also flow from the above way of thinking. "It is not monastic to . . . ." begins many sentences, some of which, seen objectively, can be quite funny. The entry in the Journal for March 20 is one example. When nuns or monks say that it is not monastic to read in bed at night, to read novels, to have a solo voice used in choir, to have even a patch of carpet on a cold stone floor, to heat a freezing building before a given date, and so on, one has to wonder what "monastic" means in this context.

If one juxtaposes this thinking with a traditionalist (as opposed to truly traditional) understanding of obedience, one then has not only all necessary guidance available in the monastery, but one need hardly make personal decisions because, as I once heard, "Our Mothers will decide for us." This becomes a return, not only to the passive "feminine"—which has a kind of pseudo-mystical sweetness—but further to the child totally guided by others. (Though, what healthy child is?) The justification for all this is found in scriptural texts about the children being the ones who enter heaven. Carried to its extreme, this can lead to a total disuse of conscience. A terrible story about religious nurses, not monastics, during the Nuremberg trials has it that they were not convicted of murders done "under obedience" to doctors and superiors because they were judged "not responsible" since they claimed they always obeyed blindly.

On the side of superiors, this kind of thinking can lead to a despotic use of power, a desire to control the thinking of others, and—in one case I know well—the idea that one can lie at will to "subjects" because all right is on one's side. The threat of totalitarianism in this domain is far too little discussed.

The "return to Paradise" archetype can lead to a refusal to deal with— or cause—conflict, all in the name of peace. So that what needs to be said, done, dealt with goes totally by the board. The Rule of Benedict has an exhortation "Not to make a false peace," but this is a sentence rarely commented on, in my experience. The distinction between true and false peace can become blurred and can excuse all sorts of appeasements.

The paschal imagery with its beginnings in death can lead to a cult of suffering that can become quite pathological. A young nun in temporary vows once said to me, "The monastic life is about suffering until one dies." Huerre writes, in a letter about love, "Some religious who thought they were on earth to suffer saw in the use of this word [love] a certain provocation, a psychological and spiritual illusion."[28] Obviously this kind of thinking can lead to an almost incredible kind of harshness—not only with oneself, but even more, with others. Some of the stories of Port-Royale illustrate this very well.

It is hardly necessary to go into the deviations possible for some of the nuptial imagery mentioned. These are actually far rarer than one would think, probably because any signs of excessively sexual or hysterical preoccupations along these lines tend to get weeded out quite early. The greater danger probably lies in the opposite direction—the development of a hard, cold, rigid, asexual way of being in the name of an understanding of "purity" that has little to do with the reality. Obviously, repressing sexuality can result in all the phenomena Freud and Jung both noted—psychosomatic illness, obsessions, compulsions, and all the rest, and none of these seem, to the ordinary observer, directly connected with their real cause. This is also a place to notice Marion Woodman's work on the denial of the feminine at work in eating disorders—and in addiction as well.[29] A superior I knew years ago used to say that religious made up for the lack of sex at table. It is also worth noting, however, that my own experience, borne out by several others, is that this denial of the feminine, notably in women, or this asexual quality seems to diminish in frequency in almost exact proportion to the seriousness with which contemplation is lived and sought in a given community . . . a possible interesting commentary on the significance of nuptial imagery.

---

[28] Huerre, 131.

[29] Marion Woodman, *The Owl Was a Baker's Daughter: Obesity, Anorexia Nervosa, and the Repressed Feminine* (Toronto: Inner City Books, 1980). Some of her other works deal with the same subject.

The whole domain of transformation can lend itself to a tendency to get into ideologies about monasticism in the ways mentioned above in both journal and commentary. If people consider it "ascetically incorrect" or "inappropriate" to do something they need or badly want to do, they can lose all freedom to follow the dictates of their own being. Monasteries that pride themselves on their ascetic practice are more prone to these problems than others. A Trappistine once wrote to me that she had thought that when the rules of silence were loosened, people would see the fruit of all those years of silence emerging in real wisdom and depth. But, in fact, she felt that the conversations were so petty that one wondered what had happened in the silence all that time.

In Jungian language, what needs to be considered here is his concept of identification with the persona. If becoming a monk or a nun is perceived as a value there is a real risk, especially for someone still projecting authority and much else onto others, that the person will build up a monastic persona that forbids all sorts of "non-monastic" behavior and even thoughts or feelings. Obviously priests, sisters, doctors, lawyers, professors can do the same. But a doctor goes home to his or her spouse where a different persona is needed. A monastic persona is an all-day affair. (Think of *Asylums* again.) One can watch an occasional young nun or monk clearly acting a part and wonder who the real person is underneath. To face the real person is to face passion, shadow material, feeling and much else. If the local ideology—or the person's ideology—perceives this as "un-monastic," the stage is set for catastrophe. An example of this was given in the journal. Obviously, a Rule based on the idea of humility would seem to be the perfect preventative for such an eventuality, but unfortunately one can fake humility, too.

If there is one monastic practice that can be a preventative for very many of these problems, it is surely the one called "manifestation of thoughts" and which is very closely akin to analysis. Of course, a tremendous amount depends on the recipient of this manifestation, but where this person is healthy, humble, and free from the deviations mentioned above, a tremendous amount of healing can take place.

Psychologically speaking, then, monasticism in general and the journal in particular can be reflected upon in terms of some basic archetypes. That all of this merely scratches the surface is only too clear. It is, however, a beginning of reflection.

PART TWO

ANALYTIC INITIATION

As was said above, years after my own experiences of religious/monastic initiation, I found myself seeking Jungian psychoanalytic training. Since I had been working in the fields of counseling and mental health, it began to seem essential to get more in-depth formation. There were two possible ways to go—the academic, i.e. a second doctorate including practical experience, or the way of analytic training. Well into "the second half of life" academe can easily seem less tempting. The heart, not the head, the whole of one's being, in fact, seems a better place to start. This, not only for the patient or client's sake—a therapist has no instruments or tools beside his or her own being—but even more for one's own sake. If a human being is like an iceberg, only one-tenth visible above water, how does one get some understanding of the other nine-tenths? What is happening down there? How much of one's life and decisions is unconsciously influenced by those depths? Still more to the point, if Augustine could say, *Noverim me, noverim te*—"to know myself is to know You, God"—what does ignorance of this deeper domain imply? Aquinas said two books reveal God, Scripture and nature. If the "nature" that is the human heart is unknown can one not write a parallel to Jerome's "Ignorance of the Scriptures is ignorance of Christ" and say that ignorance of the human is ignorance of Christ?

Observations of this kind answer the obvious question: what can Jungian training and its goals possibly have to do with monasticism? The answer is that the aim of monastic initiation, which is, in fact, lifelong, is to move into a space like the one described at the end of chapter Seven of the Rule[1]—or, earlier, in the Prologue, which speaks of running in God's ways with a heart enlarged by love.[2] Ultimately, it is a space where one is seeking God but with a greater awareness that any "distance" is ours, not God's. As Augustine, again, says, "You were with me [all along during my search] and I was not with you."[3] Monastic life is a training toward the presence of God Augustine describes.

This life involves the whole of one's being and consciousness. Therefore, as time passes and human experience grows and deepens, some insight into the mystery of the human heart is important. Some insight, too, into possible deviations on the way. Finding a language for such things helps one understand. In Catholic theological circles it has been a tradition to teach philosophy before theology on the grounds that the former gives one a human language and categories to say as much as reason can of God. Psychology performs a similar function for the human process. What is interesting about Jung's psychology is that he was able to reflect on not only the human process but a certain divine-human interaction. He attempted, with varying degrees of success, to speak of God only experientially. Can one "experience" God? asks theology. Yes and no. If God is beyond all being, perhaps no. But one experiences God's "effects"—or, as the Orthodox say, "energies," and the mystics of all faiths through the ages know well that they experience something of God.

Jung's own experience does not seem at all "mystical," but his very wide readings of the mystics and of many religious traditions gave him an awareness of these "borderline" phenomena. Almost alone in the psychological field, he integrates them into his thought. Thus, many "God-seekers" have studied him, but the process of analysis and training is much more than study: it is about the integration of one's human and spiritual experience into a unity. It is about learning to become who one authenti-

[1] See above pp. 48 and 53.

[2] *RB 1980*, Prologue, 49.

[3] *The Confessions of St. Augustine,* Edward B. Pusey, trans. (New York: Modern Library, 1949) x, 221.

cally is (individuation) with the corresponding readiness to be governed by the Self and not just the ego. Such training, when it "works" can only enrich any spiritual path. Jung's theory, of course, has its built-in limitations. As he said himself: one cannot take another where one has not gone. But it has the huge advantage of an openness to a realm other psychologies can close off, and even an integration of the material of that realm into his thought. That is a great gift.

Being admitted to the Jung Institute was not easy or pain-free. As I and several friends went through these stages, there was an awareness of something mysterious about the process. Entering into it was precisely entering into an area of risk, a liminal space, from which one would clearly emerge changed. One was indeed leaving an old, safe, known world to engage in a process whose outcome could not be foreseen. Externally one would, hopefully, be received into the community of Jungian psychoanalysts at the end. But internally what were the changes and risks in store? Who knew?

There were things to be learned on an academic level, books to be read, lectures attended. But this was the least of the process. There was one's own personal analysis: a searching in-depth experience involving work with at least two different analysts over time. There was, after passing through a prolonged admission process and testing, the twice yearly set of meetings with an evaluation committee of three analysts who took their duties very seriously and did not spare one home truths. As time progressed there was supervision of one's own clinical work, as well as evaluation of a final thesis and examination. Clearly, the elements of liminality and ordeal were present, as well as those of learning from traditions and from "elders."

And "the sacred source"? Jung saw one specific archetype, that of the Self, as the *spiritus rector*,[4] the ruling spirit of all the others, their ordering principle. He saw the movement of psychological maturation as going from a life governed by the conscious ego to a life where the Self rules far more deeply and its guidance is understood and accepted far more seriously. This is part of the process that is meant to occur through the initiation of Jungian training.

What significance can all this possibly have for people with no desire to become analysts? The answer is precisely the same as the one for monastics.

---

[4] CW IXii, par. 257.

Not everyone is called to be a monk, but the monastic archetype is a human, and not just a "monastic," experience. Not everyone is called to be an analyst but the process of analysis is a profound human experience in itself and a powerful, but not the only, means toward human maturation. Not everyone needs this means, but ideally everyone would move, through whatever means, to this end and would learn something of the importance of becoming who one is in depth on the way.

As a result, this second part of these pages will try to give a sense (rather than a description) of the initiatory process involved in becoming an analyst. Much of it parallels what happens in individual (psycho)analysis, which is indeed the essential part of the training. More, it parallels the human experience of movement toward greater maturity and, one hopes, deeper wisdom. Our culture does not value the old or old age or even wisdom. Jungian theory does value the developments of this "second half of life" including its own Night Sea Journey.

In order to make this terrain a little less unfamiliar, a few pages on the theory of becoming an analyst or therapist begin this section. They can be omitted by readers but since they are written by people experienced in training, "elders," they tell us something of what any maturing human, in his or her own sphere, needs to learn.

Section One: Theory

The opening of June Singer's article on "The Education of the Analyst"[1] can really take one aback: she makes strong demands. I have chosen her work as a single voice among the many Jungians who speak on the subject because much that she says rings very true for me. She also supplies me with a "sounding" as to what might be in the mind and heart of the "trainer" in this field.

> The education of the analyst extends beyond anything that can be verbally expressed. It is, more than anything, an experience of transformation in which one comes to know one's own soul and to befriend it. In the process, it is hoped that one may become what one really is. People enter analytic training programs with a variety of conscious motives, some from a genuine desire to help, some from an insatiable curiosity about matters of depth in the human psyche. What they learn is not necessarily what they came seeking. The education of an analyst is extremely personal. The psyche is divested of its protective coverings and laid bare in the personal analysis, which is also the training analysis. In this process one feels terribly alone, even though the analyst is standing by. The analyst-to-be, like anyone else, enters the dark nights with their dreams and the terrors of the day, alone and unprotected. But the dif-

[1] June Singer, "The Education of the Analyst" in Murray Stein, ed., *Jungian Analysis*, The Reality of the Psyche Series (La Salle & London: Open Court, 1982). Henceforth referred to as "Singer."

ference in those who submit themselves to be trained as analysts is that they know they must go through the process no matter what, and neither turn back nor be led astray. They must confront all the difficulties and demons that beset the path, if they are to become the ones who will support others in their soul-journeys.[2]

The theme of transformation is, of course, precisely that of initiation. "Becoming who one really is" involves integrating the other nine-tenths of the iceberg. It is also the central human task—so often, sadly, not fulfilled. The element of mystery, in this process as in human life, is well brought out here: "What they learn is not necessarily what they came seeking." The imagery of the night, the necessary darkness, the desert comes into focus here in terms of its purposes—for anyone.

She continues by speaking of the training as supplying a kind of map of this unknown and unknowable territory where the analyst will need to guide others. Such a map, she says, is based on stories told by people who have been in this unknown territory—experiences, myths, legends, science, faith. This sort of "map" can only be given to someone capable of self-reflection and self-examination. "The education of the analyst also creates a basic 'Jungian attitude' . . . in the analyst." Finally, the analyst-to-be must learn to balance in creative tension the opposite poles of non-conformism and readiness to be trained.

Analysis, says Singer, is a way of life. She lists the qualities necessary to go this way:

1) A sense of vocation: "one heeds the analytic calling because one must";
2) A "sense of the symbolic dimension of life";
3) Commitment to a process of growth through reading, study, self-observation, continuing analysis—as well as the ability to bear the fallow periods when for long stretches nothing seems to happen;
4) Personal integrity in the sense of taking responsibility for one's words and deeds; ability to risk being unpopular and even disliked is necessary;
5) Flexibility and ability to be oneself;
6) a genuine liking for people and acceptance of others as they are;

[2] Ibid., 367.

7) the ability to care for oneself as the only basis for caring for the other;

8) the ability to love "without possessiveness and to hate without the need for retribution" so that deep feelings can be experienced when present and reflected on ;

9) the kind of psychic energy that enables a person to take negative experience, pain, suffering in one's own life and another's without collapsing.

The qualities Singer lists are important:

- A "sense of vocation" is reminiscent of both the monastic way and the *"thwasa"* of the introduction.[3] One cannot be herded into a real initiatory process: it has to be individual.

- The readiness to grow and learn is, of course, essential to the process—and to all one's life.

- The final sections paint a portrait of a human being come to some level of wisdom and maturity. Conceivably an interesting checklist.

A single quotation sums it up well: "An analyst is needed who is not only wise and compassionate, but also singed, scorched, and seasoned: someone who understands how tough life really is."[4]

Singer speaks from a strictly Jungian perspective: another article from a less specialized viewpoint may be helpful to the interested reader. It is found in appendix I at the end of this book. In the thought of this author and in the language of initiation, the trainee therapist moves from the land or space of illusion ("I'm supposed to know it all and be perfect") with the necessary lies and secrets required to preserve such illusion, through a "desert" space where things are confusing and disorienting as reality invades the illusion, to a final space of truth—hopefully shared with other therapists. Many human experiences—parenting, teaching, relating—share such a process, and that is a possible initiatory element in each, at least where the process comes to term.

---

[3] See p. 3 above.
[4] Singer, 369.

SECTION TWO: EXPERIENCES OF TRAINING

As in the case of monastic initiation, it is important to see the Jungian process enfleshed. In researching this material I interviewed seventeen analysts or advanced trainees from six different training institutes in three different countries, hoping to get a wide gamut of experiences and find similarities and dissimilarities.

What are the main threads of these experiences and do they fit into the three stages and five characteristics of liminality mentioned above?

The three stages seem rather obvious: application, training (the liminal stage) and acceptance as an analyst. The liminal period seems a better basis for discussion. It can best be seen under four basic headings: ordeal, disillusionment, integration, and dreams.

Ordeal

There are several major ordeals during the training process, and some of these differ from institute to institute. In almost all cases, applying is an ordeal—partly because of the difficulty of being accepted, partly because of the depth of self-revelation and self-analysis involved that meets the evaluations of a committee experienced as friendly or not and extremely powerful over one's future. One person's comments give an excellent insight into one way of experiencing this ordeal. Having already reached a level of serious reflection and maturity, he came to the interviews determined to be himself in depth, whatever the consequences. Under these circumstances, being accepted brought a level of validation impossible otherwise, and this was a source of great joy. Here the theme of ordeal necessarily overlaps with that of the "elders."

For others the ordeal is an initial rejection. People apply for different reasons, or at least motivated by different inner or outer events—a shock/trauma/loss, a religious experience, an illness with its "conversion" potential, a sense of the importance of the Jungian ethos, a series of dreams (or nightmares!), a positive experience of analysis. One could go on. It is not a decision made lightly so an initial rejection can cut deep. The question is: is the sense of vocation, of need to do this, deep enough to motivate a return, a willingness to risk such an in-depth rejection again? Since all applicants are necessarily in analysis themselves, at least they have someone with whom to process this question.

Applicants are often aware that this is a plunge into a process that can change their whole lives. (One can note the parallel with monasticism.) This in itself is a challenge. What is the unknown land where one will emerge at the end of the process? And, in some cases, the decision to train *is* about "land," requiring a move to another state or even country, a total uprooting, and this at a stage of life where putting down roots and establishing security would seem most important. Once again the element of sacrifice and renunciation involved can be a measure of the values sought or intuited. And once again the parallel with entrance into a monastery or into some other crucial human decisions—like marriage, for example—is worth keeping in mind. It takes a lot of courage to decide really to live.

In more than one institute the application process can be very prolonged and can involve many very searching interviews—a real test of the applicant's mettle and resolve.

A final set of comments on admission had to do with questions asked during the interviews. When were they "too personal"? When was it important for an applicant to have the awareness of personal authority needed to refuse to answer? Even at this early stage a level of individuation is required. And here, also, the awareness of the Self speaking through dreams and other events is essential. The seeds of the final stages need already to be there as one begins.

Once accepted, the next ordeal in sight in many institutes is the Qualifying Examination without which one is often considered unready to do analytical work. Once again, this is very parallel to many of the ordeals or tests of a classical initiation process.

Most applicants have a long history of passing examinations and they set to work to study. First blow: this is a different world. Academic study is indeed important and necessary here but it is not going to get one through this particular examination. What is, then? Only what has been learned in analysis, in self-reflection, in the ability to apply theory practically to one's own process. The classical saying is: whatever your weak spot, they'll find it. And woe betide the examinee who is unconscious of it or unable to work with it him or herself, even in the presence of examiners.

The positive side of preparation for this testing is expressed in various ways:

- "I realized that I needed to do this my way, to study what I wished to learn, not to please anyone else."
- "I decided to let dreams, or the Self, guide the process and not dictate it myself."

One sees here a double theme, repeated throughout the training (as throughout many a working analysis)—the increasing awareness of personal authority and responsibility, and the increasing openness to and awareness of guidance by the Self. The experience of pulling together the threads of one's previous learnings and experiences can be extremely joyful even with the ordeal of an examination and its deep "testing" lying ahead. The prospect is rarely without some dread: who knows how it will go? And whether one will pass after years of study and reflection. But if one does, the sense of validation and acceptance by the "elders" can be extraordinarily reinforcing. And even if one does not, the experience has had great value just in itself. Normally one can always re-try.

The issue of the "elders," however, is in place well before this. One needs permission to sit for the examination and this permission is not forthcoming until it is felt that the applicant is ready. The applicant may feel unduly—and unfairly—delayed; may feel a victim of personal dislike and prejudice; may feel at the mercy of underqualified people. (One trainee said, "As I talk with X (an evaluating analyst) what keeps going around in my head is: 'underanalyzed, underanalyzed.'")

A sense of profound powerlessness—and profound anger and resentment—can develop in this situation. The ultimate, testing, question is, of course: how will this be dealt with? One can mope, fuss, complain, but none of these responses will bear fruit. (One can think of the Israelites in the desert, here, or Benedict's strictures about "grumbling.") Where is this anger meant to go? One person waited a long time and then went to her committee and said, "One can run a restive horse in small circles to contain its energy, but only for just so long. Then it *has* to find the plains where it will be allowed to run." The very successful examination that followed proved her right about readiness.

Disillusionment

In the process of analytic training there is one essential component that may not be part of the classical initiatory schema but that is in fact an essential ordeal for many a human initiatory experience, including the monastic. This is the painful process of disillusionment. The young adolescent who first comes to the painful realization that her parents are not perfect after all or the young athlete who begins to see the flaws in his coach experience the beginnings of this process. The young couple learning to deal with the reality of the other person rather than a shining projection[1] also learn it. One can enter monastic life with a dream or an idealized vision, only to find how very human, fallible, and weak are not only the other monastics but even the institution. And, fate worse than death, one learns the same about oneself. As we saw, for Benedict, as for Jung, the acceptance of this reality is absolutely essential for a real engagement in one's inner work.

For the aspiring analyst it is the same, as the two articles about theory showed. The experience, however, can involve some severe jolts. When well-respected candidates are rejected at some stage of the process; when people with some major blind spots or lacunae seem to have unlimited power in an institute, or in a person's life, the demons of experienced powerlessness and bitter disillusionment can fill one's psychological horizon. As with the early monks in the Egyptian desert, so the budding analyst must know how to deal with these demons if he or she is to emerge from training in any way ready to work. There will be scars, as in many a traditional initiation. What one does with them is the question.

[1] John Sanford, *The Invisible Partners: How the Male and Female in Each of Us Affects our Relationships* (New York: Paulist, 1980) passim.

A defense easily used by whatever "elder" is in question in some form of this experience is: "Oh well, that is initiatory." One hears this a lot. In an abusive military situation: we have to toughen these guys up. In some religious circles: we should just offer up our sufferings. In education: spare the rod and spoil the child.

The fallacy in all this is that, while in certain tribal initiations the elders really are the "initiators," there are other initiatory processes, including monastic and analytic training, that carry enough trial or ordeal elements in themselves. The "elders" really do not need to exacerbate these. Nor is it a justifiable excuse to avoid facing one's own defects, or those of the institution, just to say "Oh well, you'll just have to cope. We're the ones with the power and that's how it is." The criticisms of newcomers and those in training can be a precious purifying and enlightening element for an institution which wishes to remain alive. The refusal to listen, whatever one chooses to do with the information after real reflection, is probably the surest death warrant.

Obviously, people do not use such excuses explicitly. But "It's just initiatory" can amount to the same. Or even "That's just the way things are." On the receiving end, however, the trial is precisely: how am I going to cope with the reality that this *is* the way things are? For six or seven bad responses there may be one or two good ones. The analyst who doesn't find them won't be much use to analysands dealing with parallel situations.

Integration

At each stage of this "liminal" process, there are integrations that need to take place in preparation for the final integration into a new stage of life. We have mentioned the early learning that head-knowledge was not going to suffice for the process. Following examinations, and the experience of the importance of inner work and struggle, there can be a kind of darkness and let-down with an accompanying real distaste for study and writing. And this can occur at precisely the moment when one is asked to write case reports, a thesis, and the like.

This experience carries plenty of problems of its own. There is the trainee who discovers a whole field of interest outside the traditional Jungian mode and wants to integrate it—at the risk of being heavily criticized by his or her evaluation committee. There is the slowly growing confidence that one knows what one is doing, combined with feedback that one's work is not "according to Hoyle" (or Jung!). If, for example, those responsible for training insist on a symbolic reading of incest and sexual abuse issues, and a trainee, having experienced such trauma, wishes to discuss its reality but is accused of "concretistic" thinking as a result, that is painful to say the least. Yet such experiences are important parts of one's process.

There can be major events in one's external life—death of an analyst, illness, financial reverses, personal traumas. All of this needs to be painfully integrated if one is to be able to come out the other side. In programs where the clinical work is the focus from the very beginning and the main "test" is a prolonged analysis with one or two people, the life circumstances of such an analysand—a move or termination of analysis—can delay the completion of training for years. The ethical and emotional issues involved can be imagined!

The tensions between one's own intellectual output—papers, for example—and the possibly conflicting views of one's mentors can be another major trial requiring integration. One must be able both to stand for one's understanding and to listen well and deeply. Valuable lessons for an analyst but also for living humanly with different kinds of people.

Dreams

One of the characteristics of the liminal period was listed as contact with a sacred source. The Jungian language for this would be the relationship with the Self. One of the various ways in which one can become aware of the Self and its guidance is dreams. Several trainees or analysts were willing to share dreams concerning this time of training. A few dreams from salient moments in the process are included below. Clearly, these cannot be dealt with on a personal basis, for this is a matter for individual analysis. But some of their archetypal meanings can be appropriately discussed.

In the process of discerning whether to apply for training or not, one person dreamed:

> I am living in one of the Indian villages built on the cliff-side of a mountain in the Southwest. I have been there some time but I am beginning to learn some of the secrets of the Indians which it is death to know,

and so I think I had better escape. A kind of caravan is coming through with an old man in charge. I think joining them would be the way to go. He agrees but tells me, "You will not die from knowing these things because you are grounded in your own culture."

The dreamer took this dream as a confirmation that she should apply—taking "the secrets of the Indians" as being the mysteries of the unconscious of which she would learn more but which would not be submerging if she was grounded in who she was. The theme of death and the risk of death is closely connected with that of initiation, which implies death for the sake of re-birth. Jung speaks of contact with the Self being death to the ego.[2]

In another dream, just before the application interview, she dreamed she went to the Institute for the interview and found the waiting area full of people of all nationalities and races—an Indian woman in a sari, others in other national costumes. Once again she saw in this an indication of the universality of the collective unconscious as described by Jung.

Another candidate dreamed, the night after her first interview:

I am swimming in a river underground. It becomes narrower. My head is caught in earth. I know I have only so much time left to get my breath. It is like the birth canal.

This dream reflects what the experience of entering into training can indeed mean—the struggle of coming into birth in a new way and, once again, through a kind of death and the danger of death.

After her Stage One examinations, one candidate dreamed:

I am sitting with my examination committee, one woman who is something like X (an analyst who was on her admissions committee) and two male analysts. I talk animatedly about how much I am getting out of *Women Who Run with the Wolves*, that I didn't first like it but I do now. The woman asks me why. As I talk I move to the left. My dog Miki is with me. I have trouble talking because the sun is streaming into my eyes. I move my chair to the left, so that I am not as blind. When I do this, I realize that Miki has gone on a huge piece of grey linoleum. I must clean this up. I roll up three layers of floor covering and carry the roll up with me to get closer to water. Now they have moved and I am on the porch.

[2] CW XIV, 546.

I am very aware of my bumbling, awkward effort to cover up and clean up what my dog has done. This is not so serious. I just need to calm down, clean the shit off, and return the linoleum where it belongs. I find myself cutting a mask from the grey flooring. I am cutting carefully around circular disks that attach the flooring to snaps on the floor so that they are intact.

The dream reflects a continual movement toward the left, the unconscious, away from "head-y" talk and too bright sun (consciousness). The dreamer has been very conscious, during her time of study for the examinations, that she needed to move out of her head and to the guidance that came from "the left." I take the dog, as does the dreamer, to represent instinct and affect and, in the circumstances, it makes a mess. The dreamer's comment was: "What shit do I need to look at?" This trainee is noticeably not over-concerned with this situation (it is "not so serious"), and in fact she had reached a place in her training where she felt able to be very honestly herself, "warts and all." I believe this dream reflects a principle often repeated to trainees: what will matter in the examination is not what complexes show but how able you are to deal with them honestly. Here, the dreamer just calms down, cleans up, and goes on. The mess-making dog can also be about the question of the training of the instincts toward greater development and maturation—a process that occurs during training, one hopes, as well as during the examination process. The last section speaks of setting up a persona (mask) that is careful to be grounded and that is not flashy or noticeable but simple (grey linoleum).

Another dream shows the deep emotional pain that can be experienced when the same examination process goes negatively. The night after learning of her failure in the examination—a failure of which she was told, she felt, very coldly, a trainee dreamed:

> I was in a city at night, very dark. I am walking. I am beaten severely by two men present with a woman. They leave. I am left on the ground, nearly beaten to death. I remember the feeling in my body—especially in my stomach where I was kicked. I was left for dead.

As far as identity as a candidate or analyst goes, the examination process can be important. One trainee who had always so far dreamed of herself as a member of her previous profession, dreamed after passing the Stage One examinations:

> I am walking with my true love, a medical student, on the grounds of a hospital where he works. I ask him what he will do this afternoon. "See a patient with lower back pain," he says. "But it is you who should be seeing him, not me."

This dream caused the dreamer real joy in terms of its reflection of deep awareness of her new identity.

One could go on at length with dreams, but these give some idea of this deeper accompaniment of the training process.

It is fitting to end this section with a dream that suggests the Dream-maker's sense of humor. It occurred just before the trainee's Stage Two—that is, final—examinations.

> I am both a stage-hand and an actor in a play. There are five stages. I am preparing to work/act on the third but stages four and five are still to come.

Summary

It will have become clear from the preceding sections that the characteristics of the liminal space in initiation are very much present in the training process. The notion of ordeal was discussed extensively, notably as it interacts with that of the elders. The tradition is passed on by each institute and its "elders" but also by the extensive study of the works of both Jung and more recent theorists. The relation to the Self, also, has emerged throughout.

What is more questionable is the notion of obedience—not a popular virtue in Jungian circles. But this unpopularity may be rather more theoretical than real. Someone unable to get into the spirit of the Jungian ethos is quite simply not kept in the training programs I know. People are expected to think for themselves and come to their own maturity, but this is definitely seen as being in dialogue with Jungian thought, or why train in this specific field?

So it remains to see, for this experience as for monasticism, what underlying archetypes seem the most significant.

SECTION THREE: ARCHETYPES

One way of reflecting on some of the above experiences is by discussing a few previously mentioned archetypal themes and images, as well as one or two not yet mentioned. This process will also show archetypal connections with the material of Part One.

Night Sea Journey and the Hero's Progress[1]

The first paragraphs of Section Two commented on the ordeal of application—the suffering that often led to it, the difficulties of the process itself, the fact that it began a process that would change one's whole life, the joy of finally being accepted.

The elements of night, darkness, suffering are important here, as are the comments about change and movement into new life. I think everyone would agree that no one emerges from the training process unchanged. Rather, the psychological and even spiritual change involved is very deep.

In Part One there is a treatment of Jung's views on the Night Sea Journey, and this was seen as a central paradigm in the monastic process. There, a key concept for meeting the darkness was humility; here it is

---

[1] See Joseph Campbell, *The Hero with a Thousand Faces,* Bollingen Series XVII (Princeton: Princeton University Press, 1949, 1969). Henceforth referred to as "Campbell."

shadow. As one decides to apply, all one's self-doubt, all one's negative emotion can emerge, and doubly as one places this question in the hands of three, or more, people who can decide one's future. Without some beginning awareness of one's own personal shadow and of the shadow of others that can arise during this ordeal, the process is unlikely to go well. This experience might seem a naked experience of power, but it needs understanding in terms of these deeper elements.

The point is that it is essential to the whole process for the applicant to have centered sufficiently in his or her being to know who he or she is— shadow elements, personal authority, being, and much else. This deeply changes the whole experience. If the applicant is really ready, this whole ordeal can also be a coming to awareness of one's own power rather than of the apparent total helplessness. There is darkness and difficulty in the process because of the element of threat and ordeal. It needs, however, to be sufficiently an "heroic" journey for there to be emergence, new life, new beginning or new day from this ordeal. This is the first step in this initiatory process.

The same phenomenon is discussed in greater depth in the second major ordeal—the qualifying examinations and preparing for them. One interviewee after another spoke of the profound psychological upheavals and change that occurred both during the preparation and in the aftermath of the examinations. There is a slow realization that one needs to go into the darkness of guidance by the Self and simply trust that this will be the way. The relative lights of mastery of material, control, and intellectual centrality have to be renounced, and one simply has to learn to trust the guidance of a part of the psyche far deeper than the ego. Dreams may help, but often the whole process remains very obscure, and yet it carries its own inner coherence.

Where the experience of the examination is positive and reinforcing, this can be the beginning of a return to light, but even in this case, the psychological change that has occurred and its repercussions are sufficiently deep to keep this cyclical movement through darkness into light recurring.

Several trainees referred to dramatic events that occurred during this time, deepening the sense of night—death of an analyst, struggles for permission to take examinations, physical illness. Some spoke of "searing pain" in this darkness. Quite a few mentioned the healing experience of coming to feel accepted, of the real help received from some analysts, of a sense of new integration with the training process as the examination experience drew to a successful end.

To change the imagery, two interviewees spoke of feeling dis-membered and then put together again differently, re-membered—an experience which, it will be remembered, Eliade discusses in connection with Shamanism.[2] And so, here as in monasticism—as in many other human experiences—the Night Sea Journey is an essential archetype, one of supreme importance. One could characterize it as an essential theme of human life.

Clearly, the theme of the hero as dealt with in fairy tales and in commentaries (one thinks of Campbell as well as Jungian writers) is about this same Night Sea Journey.

In the world of myths, fairy tales, and stories, one constantly meets the image of the hero on a journey. Often he is a "dummling," rather a fool, perhaps, compared with brighter brothers, but he has a good heart. He usually has tasks to perform, a journey to make, and helpful animals and beings assist him on the way. (The masculine pronoun is used here since, despite exceptions, many fairy tale heroes are male.)

In connection with all of this it is worth remembering how more than one trainee spoke of a sense of call, of awareness of a need to leave country, work, sometimes even family to go out on the quest which seemed impossible to refuse. As in fairy tales and myths, there are ordeals and tasks. There are often very unlikely helpers from the unconscious. One trainee, badly lost in a forest in a foreign country, spoke of a little boy on a bicycle who led her back to "reality" and, strangely, to the house of an analyst who was to offer her lodging and significant mentoring.

There are dragons to slay—whether they are one's own fears or the complexes dealt with in analysis and in daily life and work. Most of the dragons turn out to be interior, but the interviewees spoke of exterior battles as well and of the growing need to come fully into one's own power and stand behind one's work.

There is more to this specific journey than the ordeals involved in thorough mastery of any field. This journey is not about acquiring exterior knowledge and power but about the obstacles that lie within. The fairy tale hero returns from his journey changed, and so does the candidate in Jungian

[2] Mircea Eliade, *Shamanism, Archaic Techniques of Ecstasy*, W. R. Trask, trans., Bollingen Series LXXVI (Princeton: Princeton University Press, 1972).

training, and so does the person undergoing any serious initiation. This is one reason not to trivialize the concept of initiation and apply it to just any human experience or achievement. If the experience of liminality with the criteria discussed in these pages is not involved, it would seem that one could question such terminology. But more of this in Part Three below.

It is commonly said of the examination process that if there is a flaw the committee will find it. In a fairy tale, also, the trials, ordeals, and journey of the hero move him or her into a place of greater strength. And so, though there is considerable mention of hurt and fear in the interviews, there is also frequent mention of obstacles conquered, of new stages of psychological life and experience reached—in other words of a process that may have been painful but which worked what it was meant to work. All this doubtless explains the comment made by one person that there is a post-initiation process of integration and healing, out of which even the scars one keeps become healed. This is a necessary completion of a difficult process or journey.

In the difficulties and ordeals of the journey the fairy tale hero has help from figures from the unconscious—dwarfs, fairies, helpful animals (though figures from the unconscious may be enemies as well). As a trainee deals with the ordeals of training, one can easily see how synchronous figures and events play their part, as do dreams.

And the analyst? Although most analysts I know would strenuously (and rightly!) object to being compared with angels, as I reflected on the role of the analyst in training, the story that came most forcefully to mind was from the Judaeo-Christian Scriptures (Tobias). A young man, son of a recently blinded father, sets out on a journey to get some money previously owed to his father. This young man, Tobias, is not far from the traditional "dummling" of fairy tales at the beginning of the story. But a young man who claims to be a kinsman offers to accompany him on the trip. As he falls in love with a maiden whose seven previous husbands were killed by demons in the bridal chamber, he is told by his companion how to avoid the same fate. He must learn to deal with the strength of his passions by a few nights of abstinence. He must burn the heart and liver of a captured fish (an element coming from unconscious depths) in the bridal chamber. The gall of the fish will heal the father's blindness.

To me, the analyst's accompaniment of the trainee while the latter deals with passions, complexes, dreams, life events and all that emerges from the unconscious is not dissimilar to what occurs in this story in terms of accompaniment, encouragement to insight, and help throughout these vicissitudes. The angel who accompanies Tobias in the guise of a kinsman is, significantly, called Raphael, "healing of God." An initiand needs such an angel or elder by his or her side during the initiation.

As always, there is the dark side. The analyst can fail the analysand—by dying, moving away, not understanding, attacking, or betraying in one of many ways. Learning to work with this exceptionally painful experience is also part of the process. It creates strong opportunities for maturation and individuation—out of the darkness and pain.

Fathers and Mothers

There are, obviously, as many variations on the experience of training as there are analysts. One analyst spoke of his experience of training as initially "an initiation into the world of the fathers," a training in thinking, study, and reflection that he felt he had previously missed. He flourished with this, but predictably, as he grew in skill and self-confidence, he found other fields of study to enrich his training and had to battle "the fathers" for his right to use and integrate them. This is another classical anthropological (even zoological!) theme from a wider field than that of initiation—the new generation growing into its power and replacing the old, perhaps, if necessary, by means of a fight for one's own right to rule or take one's own power.

Still another aspect of this archetype is about the tendency to regression with its concomitant projections and the experience of "parental" power. As was said, a very important part of the training is the relation with the analysts most responsible for training. Several trainees spoke of an experience of regression where all power was given to the institute and training analysts who surely could do no wrong. At the beginning of training many feel that they have everything to learn and can project onto the analysts, or the Institute, the perfected "finished product," or the parental images of guide, good father, good mother, and the like.

Once again, the growing experience of personal authority is important along these lines. Soon enough, however, this will clash with the experience of "parental" power. Refusal to accept papers, to permit examinations, to allow graduation, apparently unfair interpretations of personal process can all be elements here—among many others. From a trainee point of view the experience can feel like one of brute force, even abuse of power. From the point of view of those responsible for training, it can feel like taking responsibility for the quality of the training process. Alchemically speaking, this is one of the areas where the substance being worked on is transformed by the heat of the flames in the vessel and emerges changed.

Developmentally and analytically, the whole issue connects with that of disillusionment. As the adolescent painfully comes to face the reality of his or her parents' imperfection, so the trainee begins slowly to see through his or her projections onto the institute and the analysts. Flaws become apparent, imperfections abound. The more one projected the Self or the Wise Old Man/Woman, the worse the disillusionment. But if this process of withdrawal of projections moves concomitantly with growing awareness of shadow material, in oneself and in the world, what emerges is a purified and more realistic understanding of self, others, one's institute and, simply, life. The importance of this factor in the training of future analysts is evident.

A different experience of "the father/mother" is the sense of being accepted as an equal by the examining analysts at the time of the examinations, an experience on which several commented. It is like a validation by the initiatory elders and can be profoundly healing and even transforming. Many trainees spoke of the beauty of this experience—a first inkling of acceptance into the new community at the conclusion of the initiatory process.

It is worth remembering, in this connection, the comment of one interviewee that this whole experience is about coming into contact with the divine. In scriptural language, one only meets the God beyond all being by giving up one's idols—an interesting comment on projection! The negative expression of this same phenomenon has to do with the need to die. If what the whole process is about is movement from an ego-oriented way of life to one of obedience to the Self, there is no way of avoiding a death, much as one wants to avoid it.

Masculine and Feminine

An interesting place to begin treating this question is by remembering two contrasting points of view mentioned in some interviews. One spoke of creating a safer vessel for the Self in the future—wanting to work in a circle rather than a hierarchy. Another spoke of the need for both, circle and hierarchy, as both masculine and feminine are needed.

These quotations raise some interesting questions. How can an institute supply such a container and still further the initiatory process? If one uses masculine and feminine imagery, one can reflect on the thought of a feminist writer, a psychologist who speaks of "power from within" as feminine and "power over" as masculine. She writes:

> In a culture in which mastery is the realm of men, the male self comes to be identified with all that represents competence, control, adventure, spirit, light, transcendence of the body's dark demands. Yet that so-called freedom is actually denial—of the body, of feeling, of vulnerability and mortality.[3]

Does this quotation, which is meant to criticize the masculine, not rather suggest the need for both—masculine and feminine, spirit and body, transcendence and vulnerability? In Jungian language one could say that the ideal would be androgyny—the combining of both masculine and feminine traits in a harmonious way, the combining, for one example, of thinking and feeling in a good balance. One would hope that an initiatory process which aims at real maturation would have this result.

The material from the interviews does most certainly suggest the need for a more developed feminine in the training process and experience. The phenomenon of power in the wrong hands—so frequent in our culture—is doubly destructive in training. On the other hand, the ability to cope with power out of awareness of one's own, at whatever cost, is surely an absolutely essential learning for an analyst.

But in order to reflect on what Starhawk calls "power over," it is necessary to see it in terms of another archetype.

The Encounter with the Shadow

This section is deliberately placed after the previous ones. Jung places the encounter and work with the shadow as the first major work to be

---

[3] Starhawk, *Dreaming the Dark: Magic, Sex and Politics* (Boston: Beacon Press, 1982) 86.

undertaken, and so it was first introduced above under the heading of the Night Sea Journey.

This work, however, is cyclical and is always to be redone on a deeper level. In the process of reflecting relatively globally on the preceding material, one can come to several conclusions. The first is that just as the initiations in so-called primitive tribes move the subject from childhood and parental care to puberty and greater adult independence, so later initiations of the kind discussed in these pages move one into another kind of maturation on a higher level, and therein lies their half-hidden promise for the candidate. Monasticism promises a kind of initiation into wisdom. Analytic training promises a growing understanding of the psyche and its movements, of oneself, of the *humanum*.

The price of these wisdoms is to put oneself once more "in school"— the monastic "school of the Lord's service" or the analytic school with its process of training. Once again one is subject to quasi-parental figures and their power. Once again one has to work with the tendency to regress. Part of this latter tendency, if one gives in to it, is the feeling of powerlessness often mentioned in the interviews. When power is exercised over the candidate, it is easy to feel rage, fear, and all the concomitant childhood emotions. For the infant, the first absolute need is to exist. When one feels power being exercised over oneself, this can throw one into a narcissistic place where one feels it is an issue of life and death not to be controlled. And when one's narcissism is triggered, it triggers that of others. Experience after experience of rage followed by depression can however bring the increasing realization that powerlessness is an illusion, a childhood experience no longer valid now. I believe there are experiences of legitimate anger on the part of trainees. There are certainly experiences of injustice in the system, as more than one analyst knows. And there are probably insufficient ways of dealing with these. But the purpose of the process is not a sadistic torturing of candidates but rather a gradual training to deal with all these issues—shadow, rage, power, pain. These are the issues analysands face daily. They will find little help from someone who has not also fought these battles and come through them on the other side.

The darkness of shadow material recurs in wave after wave. Just when things seem quiet, another upsurge comes. But this is a major inner ordeal essential to the process. Writing this material and hearing these interviewees was about coming into touch with the "pearl" each person was seeking. But it also aroused anger and a sense of injustice in more than one situation. There are clearly issues about training that still need to be addressed and that bring one into full shadow material. As with all human issues, as we begin to make new discoveries—in science as well as psychology—we push into the frontiers of darkness, of our own ignorance and unknowing and personal shadowlands. We can misuse both knowledge and power and must struggle hard not to do either. And we must struggle when others seem involved in these same misuses. The battle with the sense of powerlessness forces us to work through it, to come to our own awareness of what we can do. As I met interviewees who were working through these issues, I learned something about possibilities along these lines. It is, in the words of the fairy tale, a "never-ending story."

And all this, in its turn, leads to a final important archetype.

The Archetype of the Self

The deepest place of analytic training certainly has to do with the movement out of an ego-controlled space into one where the archetype of the Self has its appropriate importance. Jung speaks of the Self as the center and also the circumference of the whole psyche, comprising both conscious and unconscious.[4] The process of individuation is about developing the kind of ego-Self interaction that is neither inflated—identified with the Self—nor restricted to the limits of the ego, as occurs with an immature and unintegrated psyche. The Self is the ordering principle in the psyche and also the numinous image of God in the soul. But, to Jung, the Self contains dark elements as well as light, and these must be integrated as well.

In the process of analytical training, as the interviews showed, one thing that occurs is the experience of the profound limitations of the ego and its capacities and the need to move into the deeper space ordered by the Self. One could even take this awareness as definitive of the nature of training itself. Without this experience, in whatever terms it is couched, the whole process can only fail. Several people with whom I have spoken in the course of this investigation have spoken about the tragic possibility of going through the motions exactly right; getting through the process

[4] CW IXi, 164.

somehow without being deeply scathed; and emerging without this essential, which I have called the "pearl." The same is, unfortunately, possible in monastic training. It is the saddest possible result. But no one can know whether, in fact, this is the case for anyone else. Only the depths of the psyche know. And the purpose of the process is to create precisely the opposite result, the ability to integrate the two spheres of the ego and the Self into a single, unified working whole.

PART THREE

CONCLUSIONS

After all these pages on two in-depth experiences of initiation, it is time to explore more deeply what initiation is about. This book began by posing a question: are there still in our culture initiatory experiences and, if so, what would characterize them? Having seen two such initiations of adults, it may not be amiss to look very briefly at an adolescent rite of passage in Africa.

Patrice Malidoma Some[1] was kidnapped into a Jesuit seminary as a child but escaped and returned to his tribe. He describes the initiation that followed, giving stage after stage of the process in which, by entry into the underworld, previous worlds, other worlds, the initiand becomes aware of and open to totally other dimensions of human experience. This is playing with fire—sometimes literally—and some initiands lose their lives in the process. One is reminded of the comments in Part One on the Celtic notion of "thin spaces." The other worlds, the unconscious, can be places of danger.

---

[1] Patrice Malidoma Some, *Of Water and the Spirit: Ritual Magic and Initiation in the Life of an African Shaman* (New York: Viking [Penguin], 1955).

Initiation and Obedience

In Some's book, the only way to survive the process is by absolute obedience to the instructions of the elders, who alone know the way. Barring this obedience, some initiands die. The others learn quickly from this example! Why obey, then? Because, as with Dante, only an experienced guide knows the way. Without this help one can lose everything on the shoals of illusion, danger, and fear. There is no space here for what we like to call adolescent rebellion against authority. Who disobeys the elders dies, for only they know the way, the shoals, the risks. One finds interesting parallels elsewhere.

In a totally different world, that of desert monasticism, Andre Louf writes about the same subject:

> Whenever the elders speak of obedience, what is today called the "common good" never appears on the horizon. They consider only the personal well-being of the brother who, facing his father, submits to training in obedience as he would to spiritual therapy. That is why this training demands a great deal and seems, at times, to go past the bounds of what we know to be reasonable within the normal relationships between inferior and superior in the service of the common good. This apparent excess can be understood only in the light of the psychological and spiritual development it was designed to set in motion. Some borderline cases simply set up a sort of shock-therapy that only a father can impose upon his own son, not only because he is supposed to know him better than anyone else, but above all because the son trusts him totally and feels loved. . . .[2]

Once again, the only way through the darkness and desert is with a guide. There is no other way for the initiand to move safely in what is, for him or her, still *terra incognita*. When Jung comments that an analyst can only take an analysand where he or she has been able to go, he may be referring to this same phenomenon, even though he in no way validates the notion of obedience. However, even in what has been called the twentieth-century myth par excellence, *Star Wars*, Luke Skywalker is only able to

[2] Andre Louf, "Spiritual Fatherhood in the Literature of the Desert" in John R. Sommerfeldt, ed., *Abba, Guides to Holiness and Wholeness*, Cistercian Studies Series 38 (Kalamazoo: Cistercian, 1982) 49.

become a Jedi knight through the disconcerting guidance of a most un-likely teacher, Yoda, and by unquestioning obedience to his training. In this light, some of the power issues discussed in both Parts One and Two take on a different light, though, in neither case, is an appeal made—nor would it be correctly made—to the above notion of obedience. Still, train-ing does imply learning from others who know and live what the initiand does not but wants or needs to learn. This implies inequality at the begin-ning of the process; growing equality as it proceeds; toward greater equality at the end. This is one aspect of the field we are examining. But it would seem that trying to cut this corner at the beginning of a process will skew it entirely.

It is worth mentioning, however, that in a study of Zen training we shall be looking at in appendix II below—as well as elsewhere in Zen litera-ture—this kind of obedience and submission to a spiritual master is wholly tempered by another attitude one could call deep personal independence, and this is necessary or enlightenment becomes impossible. The familiar saying, "If you see the Buddha, kill him" is clearly not about murder but about not projecting out one's own inner Buddha-nature. Jung's individua-tion process is about the same withdrawal of, consciousness of, projection.

In the light of all these examples, what could one say is meant to hap-pen in the archetypal fields through undergoing this process? I suggest that what these processes are ultimately about is going to a new level of depth in one's life. The issue is less, as in an external rite of passage, the external movement into a new community—though, in fact, in both cases we are studying this does occur. But the inner changes are by far the most important. In the monastic initiation what is involved is a passage beyond some of the most winning values of human life through a real death into a new world where all the same things appear in a different light. The Zen saying: "Before enlightenment I chopped wood and drew water; after en-lightenment I chopped wood and drew water" holds very well here. Or Merton's comment:

> The terrible human aspiration that reaches out over the abyss is calmed. The terror of God is so far beyond all conceivable terror that it ceases to terrify and then suddenly becomes friendly. Then, at last, begins the ut-terly unbelievable consolation, the consolation into which we enter through the door of an apparent despair: the deep conviction, as im-possible to explain as it is to resist, that in the depths of our uselessness

and futility we are one with God . . . . We have found Him in the
abyss of our own poverty—not in a horrible night, not in a tragic im-
molation, but simply in the ordinary uninteresting actuality of our own
everyday life.[3]

But we are ahead of ourselves. This transformation of the ordinary is the
fruit of the process we are still just describing. The first transformation is
of oneself. Let us try to speak a little more deeply about this process.

Transformation

It is interesting that one of our conclusions to the section on monasticism was that it was a "thin space" enabling "a creative transformation of
consciousness." In this case, if one were to use Jungian categories one
would say that it is about an increasing awareness of the Self and its guidance so that the personality is transformed from being ego-centered to
being guided by the Self, a very different picture. In monastic language
one would say something similar to Benedict's description of the person
transformed in love.[4]

As for the desert tradition,

> Abba Lot went to see Abba Joseph and said to him, "Abba, as far as I can
> I say my little office, I fast a little, I pray and meditate, I live in peace and
> as far as I can, I purify my thoughts. What else can I do?" Then the old
> man stood up and stretched his hands toward heaven. His fingers be-
> came like ten lamps of fire and he said to him, "If you will, you can be-
> come all flame."[5]

John of the Cross writes at length of the transforming power of fire
which first blackens a log and then turns it into flame.[6]

[3] *Silence in Heaven, a Book of the Monastic Life,* text by Thomas Merton, (New York:
Studio Publications in association with Thomas Y. Crowell) 24.

[4] See p. 46 above.

[5] Joseph of Panebysios, 7 in *The Sayings of the Desert Fathers, the Alphabetical Collec-
tion,* Benedicta Ward, trans. (Kalamazoo: Cistercian, 1975).

[6] John of the Cross, *The Living Flame of Love* in *The Collected Works of St. John of the
Cross,* Kieran Kavanaugh and Otilio Rodriguez, trans. (Washington D.C.: ICS Publications, 1979) Prologue, 7.

In his poetry, he adds:

> I begged love to kill me
> Since it had so wounded me;
> I threw myself into its fire
> Knowing it burned,
>
> Excusing now the young bird
> That would die in the fire.
> I was dying in myself
> Breathing in you alone.[7]

Why is it that Benedict, the Desert, John of the Cross all see love as the fire that transforms? Rumi will continue the theme:

> Love swells and surges the ocean
> And on your robe of stormcloud
> Sews rain designs.
>
> Love is lightning
> And also the *ahh*
> We respond with.[8]

Or

> He is the One
> Who rules the Heart and Soul in this town.
> He is the One
> Who rules like the fate of God
> Hundreds from the glory of faith
> Have fallen and worshipped in front of His face.
> Where is the cloud of doubt
> That will find the way to His moon?
> Like the darkness disappears under the moonlight,
> Hundreds of me's and you's
> Will be annihilated
> By the light of that Beauty
> Who has freed Himself from the self.

---

[7] "A Romance on the Psalm *By the Waters of Babylon*," ibid., 733.

[8] *Birdsong, Fifty-Three Short Poems translated by Coleman Barks* (Athens, Ga.: Maypop) 40.

There is no temple of peace for the destitute
But His temple.
There is no wish or desire
But the shadow of His face
Which resembles the sun.[9]

Surely, this is all mysticism—totally out of the range of what we have been discussing. But in fact the lines may be less easy to draw than would appear. The Self, as Jung sees it, the God of monasticism—Christian or otherwise—is indeed beyond the limits of human rationality. Obviously not all initiations are about coming into mystical experience. But they doubtless all involve some level of desire. The initiand's own desire (or love) is needed, even to begin the process. One can hardly be truly initiated against one's will or desire. And this desire or love needs, notably in adults, to be subsumed into a greater love than one's own. (Hence Augustine's remark about the restlessness of the human heart until it finds rest in God.)

What all this is about—whatever language one uses to discuss it—is the introduction into human functioning of another element than the human ego, an element even Jung describes as "divine"[10] though elsewhere he might rather say "archetypal." No wonder one image used is fire.

In the description of Jungian initiation, a constantly repeated theme is the primary importance of the personal analysis, the movement toward letting the Self guide one's life—whether in preparation of an examination or in writing or in behavior. That is a major reason for the emphasis laid on dreams. Once again, this is all about transformation. It is about guidance beyond the level of the ego, the conscious, the purely human. So the "thin space" imagery is rather good. There are indeed other worlds involved.

And what is the price?

Transformation and Death

A Jungian analyst who has written extensively on the phenomenon of initiation says:

---

[9] *Magnificent One, Selected New Verses from Divan-i Kebir,* Nevil Oguz Ergin, trans. (Burdett, N.Y.: Larson Publications) 18.
[10] CW VII, 403.

Somewhere between the myths of death and rebirth and the myths of death and resurrection we find abundant evidence for another theme in which the experience of death and rebirth is central—the theme of initiation. Initiation provides the archetypal pattern by which the psyche, whether in individuals or in groups of people, is enabled to make a transition from one stage of development to another and therefore brings the theme of death and rebirth into close relation to problems of education whether in a religious or a secular sense.[11]

He adds that fear of death is about "fear of change, or fear of growing up, or fear of becoming independent of the claims of the material world, or a mixture of all three." Henderson's references to death and the fear of death give us a key to the element of hardship in the above material as well as to the readiness of people to undergo it. Somehow the result seems worth the pain. Henderson's words also give us the psychological, archetypal language for what was discussed in anthropological language at the beginning of this investigation.

Jung speaks about initiation in *Symbols of Transformation* where, as Samuels comments, the issue is the death of a less adequate and the "rebirth of a renewed and more adequate condition."[12] This occurs only by contact with the numinous, the Self, and requires guidance, in most cases, to navigate the process successfully. Once again, this observation fits with what was seen above. Campbell discusses the same initiatory process and sees its stages as separation, initiation, and return.[13] He concludes that the hero is the one who has moved, through his ordeals, to a level of superconsciousness. Turner's views have already been mentioned and show the death/rebirth imagery occurring through the same three classical phases as Campbell uses.

In Jungian training it is tempting to latch onto the simple formula that one moves from an ego-directed existence to a more Self-directed one, but such language is far too facile. The reality is, once again, that one leaves one psychological domain in which one could rather comfortably live and move to a place where one has far less control, though far more openness to a language one could not decipher before and which analysis

---

[11] Joseph Henderson, *The Wisdom of the Serpent: the Myths of Death, Rebirth and Resurrection* (New York: Collier Books, 1963) 124.

[12] Samuels, "Initiation."

[13] Campbell, passim.

is a prime factor in learning. One can see why people have chosen to use death / rebirth imagery in this connection.

A further interesting illustration of this dynamic can be found in the appendix to this section with its description of the training of a Buddhist monk.

A few connected questions bear touching upon here.

Inner/Outer: Self/Other

To what degree are the initiatory processes we are discussing internal and solitary and to what degree do they need others? Throughout this paper the guidance of others has been seen as essential. And yet, paradoxically, in many ways both journeys are individual, solitary. The analyst is necessary, essential to Jungian training. The monastic tradition is passed down from father to son, from mother to daughter. But in each case the journey is also totally, ineluctably, one's own. The final external recognition, in terms of admission into the "formed" community, is only a sign of the inner process that one trusts has taken place.

Translated into other language or concepts, one has here a dialectic between oneself alone and the other(s). Neither half can be avoided. The earliest analysts, like Freud and Jung, analyzed themselves (a process frowned on now—for good reason), and, for the first analytic generations, the training was the analysis. Soon an analytic training community developed, and this brings both great contributions and real trials, as was seen. A parallel process occurs as the novice comes to know the monastic community with all its riches and foibles and finally comes to a choice that, despite any disillusionment, this is where he or she wants to live. There is, then, no way to escape solitude if this initiatory process is to take place, and there is also normally no way to do it all alone.

(There are indeed exceptional cases where someone has lived an initiatory process alone. One thinks, for example, of some early hermits—or Jung confronting his unconscious. But as one studies such cases one finds again and again that there *were* others involved. It seems to be a necessary part of the picture.)

Initiation and Mystery and Identity

In spite of the importance of the above elements, there is, as was already said, something still more important, deeper, more archetypal. The classical phrase from the *Upanishads, tat tvam asi* (that art thou—in other, awkward, words: the individual soul and the universal soul are one) has spoken to people through the ages. It will be remembered that in Part Two person after person spoke of the profound psychological change involved in training. As in the case of monasticism, one cannot wholly realize what will be involved until one enters into the process, but some mysterious factors draw one on.

One could say, again then, that the initiations we have discussed are about transformation. Or that they are about coming to awareness of the world of the unconscious, the archetypes, notably the Self, but ultimately we are also discussing personal identity, who one is. All images, conceptualizations, even symbols fall because what is involved is a living individual human and transhuman process. No two people live the same thing. And yet, Buddhism speaks of the Buddha-nature one needs to discover. Christianity speaks of one's identity as a child of God. Even Jung sees the growing consciousness of the Self as an awareness of the Christ within. This is a question of a new understanding of identity, yet not one that is foreclosed on the personal self but one that opens to a wider reality. What counts is the readiness for this openness, the readiness to undergo more than to initiate, the awareness of a mysterious Something Other whose action is ultimately more important than ours.

If the aim of the process is transformation, one soon finds, once again, that there is no shortcut to this end. One has to go through death. The deepest place in the soul, where it opens into a wider world, is found in no other way. And no one wants to die: each fights death in his or her own way, and that is some of what was described in the previous sections. Hence, again, comes the need for a guide, a "psychopomp," a tradition to lead one through the darkness—for not all deaths lead to life. And, as in Some's book, some people do not survive the process.

It needs to be understood that the guide, the tradition, does not communicate answers, for there are none. The deepest point is silence, Merton says. Hence the need to move from head to heart so frequently mentioned above. What occurs is a process and it can only barely be put into words. Nevertheless, as Campbell points out,[14] what the hero discovers is that he was of royal blood all along. The eastern Church speaks of divinization.

---

[14] Ibid., 39.

This freedom or healing is one aspect of the analytic process as well. What all myths and fairy tales and religions are about is the finding of the center where somehow time opens into eternity and meaning is found. Hence Jung's remark about the lack of any healing apart from growing awareness of meaning.[15] That central place is within—and is everywhere—and so, paradoxically, there is no possibility of a guide. But this is, nonetheless, what the processes described in this book have been about.

Identity and Individuation

Kathrin Asper begins her book *The Abandoned Child Within: On Losing and Regaining Self-Worth* with the statement: "The central concept of Jungian (i.e. analytical) psychology is *individuation*. This concept is understood as a process of 'becoming oneself' that leads the individual to a realization of the greatest possible fulfillment of his or her innate potential."[16]

Describing the purpose of monastic life, Jean-Marie Howe writes:

> Each person's being reaches to unfathomable depths. Living in contact with that depth can be a life-time endeavor or a sudden, grace-given entry into it. Depth is essential to transformation and transformation is essential to monastic life. The whole of monastic life is organized to attain this depth, without which there can be no transformation.[17]

This "depth" is about finding the space of the God-image in the soul. And individuation, also, is about relating to the "unfathomable depths" about which Howe speaks. This relationship is in itself transforming.

An interesting slant on this whole question emerges in a recent article on Christianity and Hinduism.[18] To say that Atman is Brahman (again *tat tvam*

---

[15] I have not been able to find this exact quotation. In *Memories, Dreams, Reflections* he speaks of people needing to re-find their roots to heal. In CW IXi, 293, he speaks of the archetype as a "uniting symbol" or cause of healing.

[16] Sharon E. Rooks, trans. (New York: Fromm International, 1993).

[17] "Epilogue: Cistercian Monastic Life / Vows: a Vision" in John A. Nichols and Lillian Thomas Shank, eds. *Peaceweavers: Medieval Religious Women*, II, Cistercian Studies Series 72 (Kalamazoo: Cistercian, 1987) 170–71.

[18] Leo Borelli, "Jesus Christ and Hinduism" in *American Benedictine Review* XI:1, March 1955. Ian Davie's book that the author discusses is: *Jesus Purusha, a Vedanta-Based Doctrine of Jesus* (Mass.: Lindisfarne, West Stockbridge, 1985).

asi) is also "the logical precondition of orthodox Christianity, so that just as there is an Unacknowledged Christ of the Vedanta, so also is there as Unacknowledged Vedanta behind Christianity." In Jungian language one could say that this kind of remark points toward what Jung calls the objective unconscious. Borelli adds that "it is this particular instantiation of the Vedanta premise in Jesus which makes possible its universal realization."

This reflection is not the deviation from our subject that it may appear to be. Jung's concept of the Self, according to Hannah, has roots in the *Upanishads:*

> He who dwells in the seed, and within the seed, whom the seed does not know, whose body the seed is, and who pulls (rules) the seed, he is the Self, the puller (ruler) within, the immortal; unseen but seeing; unheard but hearing; unperceived but perceiving; unknown but knowing. There is no other seer but he; there is no other hearer but he, there is no other perceiver but he, there is no other knower but he. This is thy Self, the ruler within, the immortal. Everything else is of evil.[19]

It is precisely the universality of Jungian thought along some of these lines that leads it to speak to so many people—whatever their formal religious affiliation or lack thereof. Howe's quotation sees monasticism in terms of the level of depth that Jung's language and what is here called the "Vedanta premise" point out. All of this shows a universal tendency and longing of the human heart and soul as well as the aim and deepest level of the archetype of initiation.

Is it possible to conclude to identity of thought? Of course not. Jung was deliberately heterodox in terms of formal Christianity. Hinduism and Christianity have their definite differences and a shallow syncretism serves no one's real purpose. But it is the points of contact in these traditions that are of such interest here and that illustrate so beautifully what the ultimate level of initiation is about. It is clear that there are strains of literature in both traditions that would not lend themselves to comparisons of such "similarities"—for example, on the Jungian side, positions which see the above understanding of the Self as too "monotheistic" and which prefer a

---

[19] *The Sacred Books of the East,* I, *The Upanishads,* F. Max Mueller, trans. (New York: Oxford University Press) 136, quoted in Barbara Hannah, *Jung, His Life and Work, a Biographical Memoir* (New York: J. P. Putnam, 1976) 47.

"polytheism" of attention to all the "gods" represented by whatever arises in the psyche.[20] But on the deeper level, all the above strands seem to be arrows pointing in the same direction—to the center or depth of which they all speak and where they all speak of some kind of "divinization." And, in both the monastic and the Jungian traditions, this "golden" strand is always balanced by the dark one of shadow, humility, death. They are two sides of a single experience that remains out of balance if either is lost. And they are part of an unceasing dialectic or cyclical movement into that depth or center that is more than just human. It is the place where, in Merton's language, existence opens out into the abyss of God.

[20] See, for example, James Hillman, *Re-Visioning Psychology* (New York: Harper [Colophon Books], 1975, 1977) ch. 1.

APPENDIX I:
A SECOND THEORETICAL REFLECTION ON TRAINING

"Narcissistic issues in the Training Experience of the Therapist"[1] can fill the need for a complementary non-Jungian reflection on training. Emerging from a setting in a teaching hospital, the author discusses the place of narcissistic development in the professional growth of the therapist—in a way I find extraordinarily on target.

> Kohut's (1971) analysis of narcissism and its disorders postulates a transitional developmental period between those of primary narcissism (characterized by an autistic state of hallucinatory omnipotence) and of mature narcissism (characterized by empathy, wisdom and an internalized system of goals, values and ideals). This transitional period is characterized by the ascendance and predominance of two psychological structures: the "grandiose self" which carries the sense that "I am perfect" and an "idealized parent imago" to which is attributed the sense that "You are perfect, and I am a part of you." It is to these two structures that the remnants of primary narcissistic perfection are assigned and, through a complex process of interaction with and regulation by parental and other objects, gradually transformed and refined into the more "mature" self and internalized ego-ideal.[2]

---

[1] Baird K. Brightman, "Narcissistic Issues in the Training Experience of the Therapist," privately printed. Henceforth referred to as "Brightman."

[2] Ibid., 5.

The language in this quotation is technical, but its content is very valuable. The author, following Kohut, traces development from a self-centered illusion of omnipotence to a stage of greater wisdom, empathy, internalized goals, and values. Once again one has the space one leaves behind, the space one moves toward, and, in between, the liminal stage, where one finds grandiosity and the "idealized parent imago."

The author traces the training period from a first stage of "extreme narcissistic vulnerability" to a point of greater maturity. He sees the narcissistic aspirations of the budding therapist as "(a) omniscience, (b) benevolence, and (c) omnipotence . . . together as making up the trainee's *grandiose professional self*."[3] Obviously, the experience of clinical work reveals all too quickly to the would-be therapist his or her ignorance, destructiveness, helplessness, and other professional lacunae, with the narcissistic wounding that results. And this can feel like a terrible secret that he or she hardly wants to admit to him or herself. (I remember commenting to someone who had supervised my therapeutic beginnings, "I used to think you considered me a terrible therapist" only to add sheepishly, as I heard myself say it, "Well, I was just beginning and I *was* a terrible therapist.")

This author's description of the transition through this particular initiation can be seen as significant for the normal human challenge of coming to terms with one's flaws and shadow with some degree of serenity and humility. It also clarifies a concept Jung called "identification with the persona."[4] The face one presents to the world in a given situation—as Greek actors had a mask for their parts—can become something with which one identifies to a point of forgetting who one really is, "warts and all." A wise training process—like wise guidance in life—helps one disidentify from the persona in order to become oneself.

The article lists a variety of defenses trainees use to avoid facing the darkness of their limitations. After giving the repercussions of such defenses in detail, the author adds that ideally the struggle should lead to a certain modification of goals:

> Specifically, this would entail a modification of the grandiose professional self-image of the omniscient, benevolent and omnipotent thera-

---

[3] Ibid., 6.
[4] CW VII, 193–95.

pist to a more moderate and attainable ego-ideal: a therapist who has some expertise which is limited by the state of the art, one's own stage of professional development, and the patient's capacity to form an alliance around the work; one who feels concern and caring as well as the full range of human emotions, and attempts to use them in the service of being therapeutic; and one who has sufficient strength of character to provide a degree of security and support but cannot make changes in or decisions for the patient. This mourning process appears to be the most adaptive and stable of the three recovery pathways from professional despair . . . .[5]

As in a child the movement toward a mature self-love is facilitated by good enough parenting, so, comments the article, therapeutic development is furthered by a good supervisory relationship. Trainees studied by this author were helped when a supervisor had two qualities: "(1) He/she really seemed to understand, respect, and care about me and how my training was going," and (2) "He/she was an excellent clinician whom I admired and would wish to be like professionally." In Kohutian language, empathy enables a growth in self-validation, a sense of self-worth. In more Jungian language, such supervision can supply a safe container to look at the depth of one's personal and professional insufficiencies. Winnicott speaks of the need for "good-enough mothering"[6] for a child to develop with a necessary sense of self-worth. It is not difficult to see the parallels here.

There follows a long analysis of the process of idealization as well as resistance to this on either side, trainee and supervisor. Since the idealization is an important part of the trainee's growth process, parallel to the idealization of the parent by the child, excessive defensiveness on either side can be damaging. Being too insecure, too hurt by past training, too defensive as a trainee—or too uncomfortable with this transference as a supervisor—can prevent the appropriate development of the process. Where it works, the trainee's belief in his or her own humanly limited competence grows and the need to idealize lessens. This process enables

[5] Brightman, 16.

[6] D. W. Winnicott, *The Maturational Processes and the Facilitating Environment: Studies in the Theory of Emotional Development,* (Madison, Conn.: International Universities Press, 1963) 57–58 and 145–46.

the trainee truly to relate to others, and to patients, as opposed to a previous tendency to use them to fill narcissistic needs (for mirroring or idealization). The ability to *be* used as the patient needs (rather than wants)
and still maintain personal and emotional freedom is a desirable result of
this process.

Once again, expressed in more Jungian language, one could see this
process as concerned with an acceptance first of one's own shadow and,
later, of the supervisor's (analyst's/institute's). It is also about a gradual
recognition that the professional excellence projected upon analysts and
supervisors exists in the trainee as well, albeit in different forms. Perhaps
ultimately it is about the recognition that the ego, however well-trained
and competent, is not the appropriate director of the analytic process—
neither one's own nor one's analysands.'

APPENDIX II:
A ZEN EXPERIENCE

In a book called *The Training of the Zen Buddhist Monk*[1] Daisetz Teitaro Suzuki divides his material into six chapters, followed by an appendix: Initiation, Life of Humility, Life of Labor, Life of Service, Life of Prayer and Gratitude, and Life of Meditation. While a short reflection on this material might seem to belong in Part One, it would seem, on the contrary, that placing it among our conclusions can help it to serve as a sort of summary of some important points previously discussed.

"Initiation" speaks of the monk-to-be's arrival at the monastery. He arrives walking, often many miles, dressed in the complete monastic traveling attire of old, for this pilgrimage is already part of his initiation. He will receive shelter where he finds it, from a friendly Buddhist temple or simply under the stars. He walks, keeping the fundamental questions whose answers he seeks in his heart, "keeping a close contact with life" by walking. "When this contact is lost, the questions become subjects of intellection. The young monk must, therefore, experience life in its hardest and toughest aspects; unless he suffers he cannot probe into the depths of his own being."[2]

---

[1] *The Training of the Zen Buddhist Monk* (New York: Globe Press Books), nd. Henceforth referred to as "Suzuki."

[2] Ibid., 9.

Those familiar with the writings of the Christian desert will recognize the unwillingness of those living there to theorize about Scripture or anything else. The inner journey involved is made by living it, not by reflecting upon it or talking about it. This is not to condemn knowledge: after all, Suzuki has written more than one book. But it is to warn against the defense of intellectualization which can be an excuse not to live.

The young monk arrives at his destination and knocks. But he is told he will not be received. There is no room. The monastery is too poor. And on and on. He is lucky not to be received with blows. He may conceivably be invited in as night falls, but this is not because a warm bed waits. He is expected to "sit" in meditation, facing the wall until morning when he will return outside to nod over his baggage for another day. After three to five days spent along these lines, he may be admitted and introduced to the master, but the latter's greeting and questioning may well be already full of Zen paradox. Receiving his koan will still take another wait.

The purpose of all this, and much else, as Suzuki explains is to live the need for humility. To continue the learning the monks beg their meals, dressed in hats, which prevent their seeing the face of their donor and vice versa. There would be no merit in a gift to a friend nor in a too-personal receiving. The monk receives solely because he is a begging monk and the gift is meritorious.

> When Nan-ch'uan . . . saw one of his monks washing a bowl, he took
> it away from him. The monk stood empty-handed. Thereupon Ch'uan
> remarked "The bowl is in my hands, and what is the use of making so
> much talk about it?"[3]

Is this about what the desert calls "thoughts"? Or is it about Zen paradox and "humiliation"? In either case, the issue is a certain attitude to life, events, others' behavior, one that is familiar in monastic literature worldwide. It is its own form of "ordeal" but, far more, it is about remaining in contact with *humus,* the earth.

The following chapter "Life of Labour" is a continuation of the same principles. *All* the monks work: there is no exemption for those with greater authority or dignity. It is a deliberately democratic phenomenon.

---

[3] Ibid., 24.

The Yogin may think he has clearly seen into this meaning. But when this does not go beyond his hours of meditation, that is, when it is not actually put to experiments in his daily life, the solution is mostly ideational, it bears no fruits, and therefore it dies out before long. Zen masters have, therefore, always been anxious to see their monks work hard on the farm, in the woods, or in the mountains. . . . In fact, they themselves would lead the labouring party, taking up the spade, the scissors, or the axe, or carrying water, or pulling the cart.[4]

While this is a further reflection on intellectualization, it is also about a life of ordeal, of truly hard and austere work, not of ease. This is seen as part of the process of seeking enlightenment. St. Benedict, though in a gentler document and mode, still remarks, "They are truly monks when they live by the work of their hands."[5]

What has all this to say about other, non-monastic, forms of initiation? Much. For, once more, it is about the fact that seeking an easy way is likely to miss the end as well—a very hard lesson in our contemporary comfort-seeking American culture. One Benedictine novice master commented that he would like to send novices on a vision quest or a wilderness journey. This is not, however, something easy to explain to most communities today. When one enters Jungian training people say, "Good grief, why would you put yourself through all that." One can only answer, rather in a Zen mode, "If you don't know, I can't tell you."

Let us continue for a bit our walk with Suzuki. The chapter on the Life of Service discusses cooking, caring for the sick, washing and patching clothes, scrubbing another's back in the bath-house, cleaning the lavatories, and the like. One thing stressed is the need to value everything—not to waste even a drop of water, to use food discarded by markets but partly redeemable. Long before ecology, reverence for the environment was valued here. "In the monastery . . . monks are disciplined to take up whatever work that is assigned to them without a murmur and to do it in the best possible manner." The ability to do any work well and carefully, ready at any time to be asked, "Where are your thoughts," may well be the background of the tea ceremony that is also part of Zen monastic life.

---

[4] Ibid., 33–34.
[5] *RB 1980*, 48:8.

It resembles Benedict's treating every object in the monastery like a vessel of the altar.[6] Had Western culture developed more of this attitude we might be in less of an ecological crisis!

The following chapter on prayer rings the same notes as much in Jung's fundamental thought:

> The life of prayer begins with confession . . . raised when the devotee feels something lacking in himself and seeks to complete himself either through an outside power or by digging deeper into his own being; and the confession consists in frankly recognizing this fact which is in some cases felt as sinfulness. In Buddhist terminology, this means to grow conscious of the heaviness of one's own karma-hindrances . . . . When the devotee is innerly impelled to become conscious of this, he prays.[7]

It is, then, a question of consciousness, of becoming more aware of one's darkness and evil tendencies, rather than hiding from these awarenesses. It is interesting that for Jung the first stage of analysis is confession[8] and growing awareness of the shadow—and that ancient Christian monasticism so treasured the manifestation of thoughts.

The initiation we are discussing here, then, is not a matter primarily of external practices, even if for younger people the ordeals may be more exterior. (Though even then, one wonders . . . .). The first essential trial is the confrontation of the darkness within oneself in all honesty and openness, wherever that may lead. Once again, this is the opposite of the tendencies of our culture to hide from any self-awareness in television, computer games, if not in drugs, sex, and whatever other distraction may be available. Suzuki lists the prayers and admonitions the monk recites to keep himself on the right track, but we must resist the temptation to quote them all. The reading of the sutras is another part of this set of exercises and, once again, enables the monk to center his mind on the essential teachings.

The final chapter on meditation begins by describing the *zendo* or meditation hall. Here the monk has his own place where he also eats and sleeps. When he rises, after perhaps six and a half hours of sleep, he folds

[6] Ibid., 54:10.
[7] Suzuki, 73.
[8] CW XVI, 55ff.

up his mat, puts it on the shelf, goes to wash (using economy with the water), and returns to meditate. These details indicate once again the extreme frugality of the monk's life. All his belongings can be contained in a box a foot square. His bed simply rolls up and is stowed away.

What are the psychological repercussions of living this way? An experience of Japanese culture would suggest that it teaches reverence for the smallest flower, bush, stone. The first kernels of rice in one's bowl are offered up. One does not treat anything lightly. Native American hunting customs show something of the same spirit. If one killed a buffalo, one prayed to it first and treated it with reverence. For Native Americans finding a field of slaughtered buffalo, only parts of which were used, was a true atrocity against nature. And justifiably. Perhaps nature herself is beginning to show us why.

A brief discussion of *koans,* of meetings with the Master or *Roshi,* of the tea ceremony follows.

Finally,

> The Zendo life is considered finished not only when the truth of Sunyata is intuitively grasped, but when this truth is demonstrated in every phase of practical life . . . and also when a great heart of Karuna (love) is awakened in the way the rain falls on the unjust as well as the just, or in the way Chao-chou's stone bridge is trodden on by all sorts of beings— by horses, donkeys, tigers, jackals, tortoises, hares, human beings, etc. This is the greatest accomplishment man can achieve on earth, and every one of us cannot be expected to be capable of this; but there is no harm in our doing the utmost to approach the ideal of Bodhisattvahood . . . . When something of this ideal is firmly grasped, the monk takes leave of the Zendo and begins his real life among his fellow-beings, as a member of the great community known as the world.[9]

The implication is, of course, that the monk has "graduated," and Suzuki does indeed use this term. Is there any parallel with Benedict's thought that a monk can go into total solitude as a hermit only after being trained by the life with his brethren? Perhaps. But for our purposes what is more interesting is that this notion of "graduation" implies that the whole previous process was seen as one long initiation.

---

[9] Suzuki, 115.

As was previously said, it is important to distinguish adult initiations of this type from the rites of passage appropriate for, say, an adolescent. But as was also said, seeing the adult versions of initiation can be like looking at the whole process through a magnifying glass to see its essential elements. The number of human beings who will become Zen monks is, of course, extremely limited: this is not a common call. But the very simplicity and starkness of the process as described by Suzuki can give us greater clarity about what is involved. Being ready to handle hardship and be stripped of all non-essentials, being able to live with the greatest reverence for every object and being one finds on the earth, being open to learning from the sources of tradition meant to help one's process—all these elements echo the descriptions of liminality with which our study began.

The purpose of it all is, indeed, the contact with whatever the Zen monk is seeking in terms of enlightenment and compassion. In the West we may call it a sacred source. A Zen monk, if asked, will answer "Mu!," Nothing. But Suzuki gives us a key to what that might mean. Once again, then, we have seen, almost experientially, what the process of initiation can—and probably needs to—involve, in whatever form. Henderson spoke of death in order to live. Suzuki puts flesh on those bones. Every initiand has his or her own form of death but there is no way of economizing on this aspect of the process either. Nor is the new and different life that emerges ever to be forgotten if one is to understand.

Subject Index

Anthropological view of journal, 38–40
Analyst, education of, 63–65
Apatheia, 50–51
Archetypes, in monasticism, 40–55

Bernard of Clairvaux, 38

Cassian, 37–38
Celibacy, 37, 51
Confession, 102

Disillusionment, 67–68
Divine child, 46
Dreams, 69–72

Fathers and mothers, 77–78
Feminine, denial of, 57–58, 78–79

Hero, 75–76
Humility, 46, 51, 100

Individuation, 92–93
Initiation,
    in anthropology, 3–6
    monastic views on, 29–35

Integration, 68–69
Liminality in Jungian training, 59–60
Liturgy and archetypes, 44–45

Masculine and feminine, 78–79

Narcissism in training, 95–98
Night Sea Journey, 42, 48–49, 73–75

Obedience, 35–37, 84–85
Ordeal, 64–67

Pannikar, Raimundo, 34
Parallels between Jungian and
    monastic thought, 40ff.
Paschal Mystery, 41–42, 44–45
Psychological reflection on
    monasticism, 40–55

Return to paradise; in monastery, 43,
    49–51

Sacred marriage, 45, 51–52
Self: passim and, 81–82
Shadow, 41–42, 79–81
Shamanic training, xiv–xvi

Transformation: passim and, 86–90

Work, 100–102

Zen monastic training, 99–104